Ethiopia Health Extension Program

A WORLD BANK STUDY

Ethiopia Health Extension Program

An Institutionalized Community Approach for Universal Health Coverage

Huihui Wang, Roman Tesfaye, Gandham N. V. Ramana, and Chala Tesfaye Chekagn

WORLD BANK GROUP

Contents

Boxes

Figures

Tables

Preface

In 2011, Japan celebrated the 50th anniversary of achieving universal health coverage (UHC). To mark the occasion, the government of Japan and the World Bank conceived the idea of undertaking a multicountry study to respond to this growing demand by sharing rich and varied country experiences from countries at different stages of adopting and implementing strategies for UHC, including Japan itself. This led to the formation of a joint Japan–World Bank research team under the Japan–World Bank Partnership Program for Universal Health Coverage. The Program was set up as a two-year multicountry study to help fill the gap in knowledge about the policy decisions and implementation processes that countries undertake when they adopt the UHC goals. The Program was funded through the generous support of the government of Japan. This Country Study on Ethiopia is one of the 11 country studies on UHC that was commissioned under the Japan–World Bank Partnership Program. The other participating countries are Brazil, France, Ghana, Indonesia, Japan, Peru, Thailand, Turkey, and Vietnam.

Acknowledgments

This paper was prepared for the Japan–World Bank Partnership Program for Universal Health Coverage, with funding from the Government of Japan under the PHRD grant (TF011551). The authors appreciate the valuable comments received from the Federal Ministry of Health in Ethiopia, Netsanet Workie (Senior Economist, GHNDR, peer reviewer), and Jorge Coarasa (Senior Economist, GHNDR, peer reviewer). The authors also appreciate valuable guidance received from Abdo S. Yazbeck (Acting Practice Manager), Qaiser Khan (Program Leader) and Guang Zhe Chen (Country Director for Ethiopia).

The paper was edited by Shazia Amin, World Bank Consultant.

About the Authors

Huihui Wang, M.D., Ph.D., is a Senior Economist at Health, Nutrition and Population Global Practice, the World Bank Group. She holds a medical degree from Beijing Medical University (now known as Beijing University Health Science Center), an M.A. degree in economics and a Ph.D. degree in health services and policy analysis from University of California, Berkeley. She has more than 15 years of working experiences in the area of Universal Health Coverage. Her current responsibilities in the World Bank are managing operational and analytical advisory tasks related to health financing and service delivery in African countries. Prior to joining the World Bank, she worked on health sector reform initiatives in both China and the United States, including health financing, cost containment, health insurance benefit package and provider payments, as well as knowledge and behavioral responses to health insurance.

Roman Tesfaye Mebrahtu, M.A., is a consultant at Health, Nutrition and Population Global Practice based at the Ethiopia Country Office. She has an M.A. degree in Organizational Leadership from Azusa Pacific University, USA, and a B.A. in Business Management from Addis Ababa University. She also has a Certificate in Health System Reform and Sustainable Financing from Harvard University. Prior to her current job, she had been working in different government organizations at different capacities for about 24 years, the most recent ones being Director General of the Ethiopian Health Insurance Agency and Director General of policy, planning, resource mobilization and finance General Directorate in the Ministry of Health. She was also in charge of overall coordination of harmonization and alignment as well as partnership in the Ethiopian health sector, coordinating Development Projects & Budget in the Economic Development Bureau of Tigray Region, a Sub city manager in Addis Ababa City Administration, and a Head of the civil service reform program.

Ramana Gandham, M.D., is a Lead Health Specialist and Program leader for the World Bank Country Office of Kenya, Rwanda, and Eretria. As a program leader, he is responsible for facilitating coordination between the Country Management Unit and Global Practices for Health, Education, Social Protection, Agriculture and Environment, including the cross cutting themes of gender and donor coordination. He has been leading health sector policy dialogues and lending operations in several countries in the South Asia and Africa Region, particularly Ethiopia, India, and Kenya during the past 15 years. For example, the first Program-for-Results operation in Ethiopia; the Health Policy Forum held in Nairobi during March 2014; joint work with IFC on Health Insurance Subsidies for the Poor; technical support for leasing medical equipment in Kenya; innovative direct cash transfer programs to facility management committees in Kenya; and regional capacity building initiatives to promote governance and increase accountability in the health sector.

Chala Tesfaye Chekagn is currently working in the Ministry of Health, Ethiopia as Assistant Director of Health Extension and Primary Health services. Prior to his current position, he had been working as a program officer and team leader over the last five years. He had also worked as team leader of Health System Special support in the Ministry of Health. Chala has a B.Sc. degree from Jimma University and he is currently taking Master courses in General Public health.

Abbreviations

ARI	acute respiratory infection
ARM	Annual Review Meeting
BCG	Bacillus Calmette-Guérin
BOFED	Regional Bureau of Finance and Economic Development
BP	blood pressure
CBHI	Community-based Health Insurance
CDC	Centers for Disease Control and Prevention
CSDH	WHO's Commission on Social Determinants of Health
DHS	Demographic Health Survey
DPT	diphtheria, pertussis, and tetanus
EDHS	Ethiopia Demographic and Health Survey
EHIA	Ethiopian Health Insurance Agency
EIO	Ethiopian Institution of the Ombudsman
FANC	focused antenatal care
FMHACA	Food, Medicine and Health Care Administration and Control Authority
FMOH	Federal Ministry of Health
FTA	Financial Transparency and Accountability
GAVI	Global Alliance for Vaccines and Immunization
GDP	gross domestic product
GOE	government of Ethiopia
GRM	grievance redress mechanism
GTP	Growth and Transformation Plan
HDA	health development army
HEP	Health Extension Program
HEW	health extension worker
HIV/AIDS	human immunodeficiency virus/acquired immunodeficiency syndrome
HNP	Health, Nutrition and Population

HSDP	Health Sector Development Program
ICCM	Integrated Community Case Management
IDA	International Development Association
IMCI	integrated management of childhood illness
IUD	intrauterine device
JCCC	Joint Core Coordinating Committee
JCF	Joint Consultative Forum
LAM	Lactational Amenorrhea Method
LLIN	Long-lasting Insecticidal Net
MDG	Millennium Development Goal
MDGPF MDG	Performance Fund
MOFED	Ministry of Finance and Economic Development
MOH	Ministry of Health
NHA	National Health Account
NTQF	National TVET Qualification Framework
ORS	oral rehydration solution
ORT	oral rehydration therapy
PBS	Promotion of Basic Services

Overview

Study Objective

As a low-income country, Ethiopia has made impressive progress in improving health outcomes. The Inter-agency Group for Child Mortality Estimation reported that Ethiopia has achieved Millennium Development Goal (MDG) 4, three years ahead of target, with under-five mortality at 68 per 1,000 live births in 2012.

Since the Health Extension Program (HEP) was introduced as a strategy to move toward universal health coverage (UHC) in Ethiopia, this study will examine the following:

- How HEP has contributed to the country's move toward UHC
- How other countries may learn from Ethiopia's experiences of HEP when designing their own path to UHC.

Health Extension Program

Overall Introduction

The HEP is one of the strategies adopted by the government of Ethiopia (GOE) with a view to achieving universal coverage of primary health care among its rural population by 2009, in a context of limited resources. The overall goal of HEP is to create a healthy society and to reduce maternal and child morbidity and mortality rates. The HEP is a flagship program of GOE. It was launched by the Federal Ministry of Health in 2003 in the four big agrarian regions, and then expanded to pastoral communities in 2006, and to urban areas in 2009.

This is a program that is deeply rooted in communities, providing primary-level preventive activities to household members. The program encourages families to be responsible for their own health. In addition to community activities, HEP also provides health post–based basic services, including preventive health services such as immunizations and injectable contraceptives, and limited basic curative services such as first aid and treatment of malaria, intestinal parasites, and other ailments. Case referral to health centers (HCs) is also provided when more complicated care is needed.

The services provided under HEP include 16 essential health packages under four major program areas:

- *Hygiene and environmental sanitation:* (1) proper and safe excreta disposal system, (2) proper and safe solid and liquid waste management, (3) water supply safety measures, (4) food hygiene and safety measures, (5) healthy home environment, (6) arthropods and rodent control, and (7) personal hygiene.
- *Disease prevention and control:* (1) HIV/AIDS prevention and control, (2) TB prevention and control, (3) malaria prevention and control, and (4) first aid.
- *Family health services:* (1) maternal and child health, (2) family planning, (3) immunization, (4) adolescent reproductive health, and (e) nutrition.
- *Health education and communication:* Cross cutting.

The HEP benefits from close collaboration with technical vocational education training (TVET) institutions under the Ministry of Education. The TVET institutions provide theoretical training for deployed health extension workers (HEWs). In addition, TVET institutions develop a health extension service occupational standard. In this standard, each distinct work activity is defined as a Unit of Competence, with detailed documentation in standard format about the following contents:

- *Occupational title and National TVET Qualification Framework (NTQF) level*
- *Unit title*
- *Unit code*
- *Unit descriptor*
- *Elements and performance criteria*
- *Variables and range statement*
- *Evidence guide.*

Context

The HEP was developed with full recognition of Ethiopia's macro resource constraints. It was developed in a context where health outcomes and coverage of essential services were very poor, and there was a large disparity between rural and urban populations, and between better-educated and less-educated people.

The HEP, initiated and led by GOE, was designed on the basis of experiences and challenges in the earlier community health workers' initiatives, such as those involving traditional birth attendants and other voluntary workers. In addition, there has been South-South cooperation and experience-sharing with Kerala State, India.

Key Actors

As key vehicles for the implementation of the HEP, HEWs were deployed to *kebeles* (villages); model families were trained in communities; and the health development army was mobilized. Together, they form key forces for the implementation of the HEP.

Health Extension Workers: The HEWs are the key drivers of the program. Two HEWs are deployed for each health post serving 3,000 to 5,000 population. They are recruited based on nationally agreed criteria that include residence in the village, capacity to speak local language, graduation from 10th grade, and willingness to remain in the village and serve communities. Selection is done by a committee comprising members nominated by the local community and representatives from the *woreda* (district) health office, the woreda capacity-building office, and the woreda education office.

Model Families: Model families are those households that are (1) trained in maternal health, malaria prevention and control, and hygiene and environmental sanitation packages; (2) able to implement these packages after the training; and (3) able to influence their relatives and neighbors to adopt the same practices. Before the introduction of the health development army, model families were expected to gather regularly for experience sharing. They now work as part of the army to engage communities for health improvement.

Health Development Army: The health development army (HDA) refers to an organized movement of communities forged through participatory learning and action meetings. The army is designed to improve the implementation capacity of the health sector by engaging communities to identify local challenges and corresponding strategies. It is also designed for scaling up best practices from one part of the country to another. A functional HDA requires the establishment of health development teams that comprise up to 30 households residing in the same neighborhood. The health development team is further divided into smaller groups of six members, commonly referred to as one-to-five networks. Leaders of the health development teams and the one-to-five networks are selected by their team members. The main criteria for selection of leaders are whether individuals belong to a model family, are trusted by team members, and are able to mobilize communities. The formation of health development teams and one-to-five networks is facilitated by HCs, HEWs and *kebele* administrations. A women-centered HDA approach was initially piloted in Tigray region, and gradually scaled up in all regions.

Financing

HEP is mainly financed by two sources: the government and communities. The government finances the program by covering salaries of all HEWs, and is responsible for management and supervision of the program. Communities' financial contribution to the program is often not in monetary form, but rather in in-kind contribution such as labor, food, and accommodation. One significant element of HEP cost is salaries for HEWs. The cost of HEWs is Br 7.5 or US$0.38 per capita.[1] A comparison of the payroll bill for HEWs with overall government health expenditure[2] shows that the salary payment for HEWs accounts for 21 percent of recurrent expenditures, and 32 percent of the woreda-level recurrent expenditure, though with large variations between woredas.

Ethiopia Health Extension Program • http://dx.doi.org/10.1596/978-1-4648-0815-9

Significant resources are needed to train model families and to establish HDA, but there is lack of data on the cost for such activities. HEWs were surveyed to estimate average total cost incurred by a household to become a model family; the overall mean cost of becoming model families for those *kebeles* was Br 871. This translates to Br 10.8 billion or US$568 million for the 12 million model families that have been trained.

HEP-UHC Conceptual Model

This study uses a general framework on social determinants of health to motivate a HEP-UHC conceptual model (figure 0.1) that examines how HEP has

Figure 0.1 Health Extension Program and Universal Health Coverage Model in Ethiopia

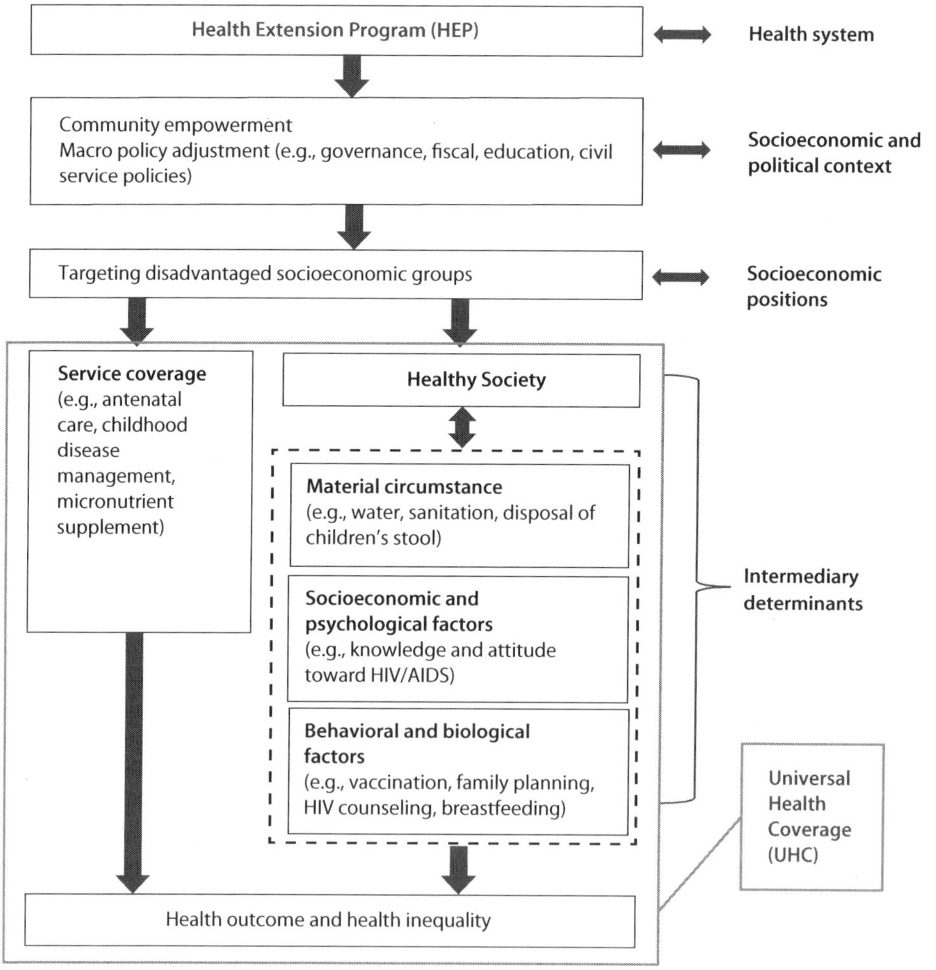

Source: Authors generation.
Note: AIDS = acquired immune deficiency syndrome; HIV = human immunodeficiency virus.

contributed to the country's move toward UHC. UHC is reflected in this framework through the following aspects: (1) creation of a healthy society measured by intermediary determinants such as circumstance factors, socioeconomic and psychological factors, and behavioral and biological factors; (2) improvement in coverage of services that minimize effects of life events; and (3) level and inequality of health outcomes.

Methods

A quantitative analysis is undertaken to understand how HEP has contributed to achieving UHC; lessons for other countries are based on existing literature. For the quantitative analysis, relative changes of a set of key indicators were estimated for the period from 2005 to 2011. This period is selected because there are population-based data available for these two years, and this timeframe can roughly reflect the situation before and after the introduction of HEP. In addition to relative changes, concentration curves are also plotted for key indicators for these two years, to demonstrate changes in wealth inequality over time. The key indicators include (1) HEP direct outputs, (2) material circumstances, (3) socioeconomic and psychological circumstances, (4) behavioral and biological factors, (5) coverage of services minimizing consequences of disease and life events, (6) proxy indicators for counterfactual situation.

Results

Under the HEP, more than 30,000 HEWs have been deployed, about 70 percent of households have graduated as model families, and more than 400,000 HDA groups were mobilized. HEWs have served a major role in training model families, facilitating HDA mobilization, disseminating health information, and providing basic services. Table 0.1 presents specific results of HEP direct outputs.

Table 0.1 Summary of Results: Health Extension Program Direct Outputs

HEP direct outputs	Results
Number of HEWs deployed	34,382 (2009/10)
Number of model families trained and graduated	12,178,630; 70.5% of all households (2010/11)
Number of HDA mobilized	442,755 HDA groups
Number of latrines constructed	2,289,741 one-to-five networks (2013/14)
Documentation of HDA activities	See box 3.1
Dissemination of family planning messages	37% through community events
Outpatient services provided by HEWs (%)	35
Contraceptives provided by HEWs (%)	24
Antenatal services provided by HEWs (%)	17
Fever treatment services provided by HEWs (%)	8
Contraceptives disseminated by HEWs (%)	12

Source: Data compiled from all the tables and figures in chapter 3.
Note: HEP = Health Extension Program; HEW = Health Extension Worker; HDA = Health Development Army.

While the HEP has been implemented, there have been impressive improvements in material circumstances; socioeconomic, psychological, behavioral, and biological factors; and coverage of services, minimizing consequences of life events and diseases. As summarized in table 0.2, most indicators have experienced changes that are pro-rural, pro-less-educated, and pro-poor, and consequently, the concentration index has decreased, and concentration curves have moved toward a more equitable situation. In table 0.2, green cells indicate positive results, meaning the relative change for rural/no education/lowest wealth quintile group is larger than the average, and the concentration curve has moved toward a more equitable scenario. On the other hand, red cells indicate the opposite, meaning the relative change for rural/no education/lowest wealth quintile group is less than the average, and the concentration curve has moved toward a less equitable scenario.

Contribution of HEP toward UHC

It is challenging to make a precise estimation of the impact of HEP on progress toward UHC because there is no counterfactual information available for comparison purposes, when a national program is under discussion. The contribution of HEP to UHC, however, can be validated through a number of perspectives that are described below.

First, there are expected changes at each link of the results chain and among the underserved population groups targeted by HEP, as shown in chapter 3. For example, at the results chain of reducing wasting, chapter 3 documents increase of improved sanitation facilities, increase in women's knowledge of properly dealing with children's stool and on using oral rehydration solution (ORS) for children with diarrhea.

Second, HEWs have served as a major source of health information (for example, family planning message) and service provision including antenatal care, family planning, and general outpatient service (including fever and diarrhea treatment).

Third, the HEP is the most important intervention undertaken in Ethiopia. There are no alternative interventions that have produced such improvements in material circumstance, knowledge and behavioral factors, and in service coverage and outcomes, particularly in rural areas and among poor people.

Lessons for Other Countries

The Ethiopian government designs and implements the HEP as a living program with different focus at different stages. The HEP builds the work program on the basis of previous achievements so that it can be raised to the next level. Figure 0.2 shows different focus of the HEP over time. First, the HEP started with deployment of HEWs in rural areas after initiation; midway in the deployment in 2007/08, HEWs began training of model families; again, when training of model

Table 0.2 Summary of Results: Intermediary Factors

	DHS results (%)		Relative changes from 2005 to 2011 (%)				Concentration indexes		
	2005	2011	Overall	Rural	No education	Lowest wealth quintile	2005	2011	Pro-equity change
Material circumstance									
Proper disposal of children's stools	21.3	35.8	68.1	69.2	78.0	132.5	0.156	0.120	Yes
Psychological environment									
Women having heard about HIV/AIDS	89.9	96.5	7.3	8.6	9.8	16.3	0.017	0.006	Yes
Women having knowledge about HIV-prevention methods	34.6	43.2	24.9	35.0	31.1	69.8	0.108	0.066	Yes
Women with accepting attitudes toward those living with HIV/AIDS	10.7	17.1	59.8	141.9	132.4	120.0	0.255	0.184	Yes
Biological and behavioral factors									
Women currently using modern contraceptive methods	13.9	27.3	96.4	112.3	122.4	225.0	0.192	0.063	Yes
Women currently using modern contraceptive methods (2014 data)[a]	13.9		190.6	250.9	253.1	577.5			Yes
Children with full vaccination	20.4	24.3	19.1	14.0	16.9	19.1	0.083	0.115	No
Initial breastfeeding within one day after birth	85.7	80.2	-6.4	-7.4	-8.4	-15.2	0.001	0.016	No
Intake of iron-rich food	11.3	13.3	17.7	20.2	16.7	33.3	0.111	0.096	Yes
Children given vitamin A supplements	45.8	53.1	15.9	18.0	15.5	14.4	0.034	0.024	Yes
Services minimizing consequences of life events and diseases									
Pregnant women receiving antenatal care	27.6	42.6	54.3	54.0	56.2	97.6	0.141	0.104	Yes
Pregnant women receiving antenatal care (2014 data)[a]	27.6	58.4	111.6	130.0	129.5	244.1			Yes
Pregnant women receiving HIV counseling during antenatal care	3.1	13.6	338.7	394.1	373.3	1666.7	0.275	0.220	Yes
Skilled birth attendance	5.7	10.0	75.4	53.8	100.0	142.9	0.314	0.304	Yes
Skilled birth attendance (2014 data)[a]	5.7	15.5	171.9	250.0	226.1	542.9	0.314	0.249	Yes
Children with fever seeking care from health providers	17.5	24.2	38.3	43.6	68.5	48.1	0.115	0.087	Yes
Children with ARI seeking care from health providers	18.7	27.0	44.4	44.5	59.7	-16.7	0.061	0.127	No
Mothers with knowledge of oral rehydration solution (ORS)	46.2	65.2	41.1	44.5	43.5	34.1	0.057	0.046	Yes

Source: Data compiled from all the tables and figures from chapter 3.

Note: AIDS = acquired immune deficiency syndrome; HIV = human immunodeficiency virus; ARI = acute respiratory infection.

a. 2014 data are available for three indicators (coverage of antenatal care, skilled birth attendance, and contraceptive use). Therefore, 2014 data are cited in the column for 2011 for these rows to compare with 2005 data.

Figure 0.2 Focus of the Health Extension Program over Time

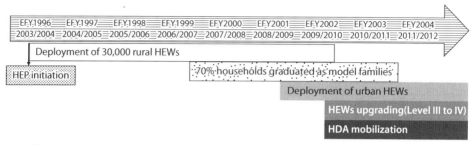

Source: Authors' compilation based on various government documents.
Note: Each colored block is a graphical representation for the period when the majority of the initiative took place.
HEW = Health Extension Worker; HEP = Health Extension Program; HDA = Health Development Army.

families was halfway through, deployment of HEWs to urban areas was started; then when deployment of HEWs and training of model families neared conclusion, upgrading of HEWs and mobilization of HDA was begun in 2010/11. Evidently, HDA formation centers on model families and relies on facilitation by HEWs.

The HEP in Ethiopia has demonstrated that an institutionalized community approach is effective in helping a country make progress toward UHC. The element of community mobilization identifies community priorities, engages and empowers community members, and solves local problems. The element of institutionalization, on the other hand, addresses the challenge of unsustainability faced by many community programs by ensuring high political commitment, coordinating national policies, and leveraging support from partners. All these may offer valuable lessons for other countries that struggle with similar challenges in the health sector.

The HEP is a program deeply rooted in communities. It encourages families to be responsible for their own health by promoting knowledge dissemination and adoption of hygiene practice, feeding practice, appropriate health-seeking behavior from professionals, and proper environmental management. This community outreach ensures a sense of ownership and sustainable changes in communities.

The implementation of HEP benefited from broad community empowerment activities under the Promotion of Basic Services (PBS) supported by multiple development partners including the World Bank. PBS supports a variety of measures designed to improve service quality and local government capacity to manage basic services.

The HEP evinces the long-term commitment of the government of Ethiopia to achieving universal health coverage. From its inception in 2003/04, it has lived through three changes of leadership in the Ministry of Health and one in the leadership of the country itself. Related issues are regularly reviewed and discussed through platforms between Federal Ministry of Health (FMOH), development partners, and regional health bureaus (RHBs).

The HEP has been seamlessly integrated into the public health system and sector management. HEWs have formed the foundation of the pyramid of the public health system. Annual Review Meetings of the health sector, as an important process of assessing past years' performance and planning next year's work, always include the HEP as one important component.

A set of coordinated national policies is indispensable for the success of the HEP. These include devolution policy that passes power to the local level for service delivery; civil service policy that mandates HEWs are recruited as civil servants; vocational education policy that makes it possible to do large-scale vocational training in short periods; and health policy that introduces HEWs as a new cadre and equips them with hardware through capital investment.

Notes

1. The monthly salary is assumed to be Br 1,500, based on the FMOH data specifying that the average monthly salary for a level IV HEW is Br 1,472. Per capita cost estimation uses the population size of 84 million. Exchange rate used is US$1 equivalent to Br 19.
2. 2010/11 government health expenditure data are used.

CHAPTER 1

Country and Sector Context

Overall Country Context

With an area of 1.1 million square kilometers and a population of 91.7 million in 2012, Ethiopia is the second-most populous country in Sub-Saharan Africa. The vast majority of the population (83 percent) resides in rural areas of the country. The economy has been growing at twice the rate of the Africa region; between 2004 and 2011, annual gross domestic product (GDP) growth averaged 10.6 percent per year compared to 5.2 percent in Sub-Saharan Africa (World Bank 2012). Economic growth brought positive trends in reducing poverty, in both urban and rural areas. While 38.7 percent of Ethiopians lived in extreme poverty in 2004/05, five years later this number was 29.6 percent, which is a decrease of 9.1 percentage points as measured according to the national poverty line of less than US$0.6 per day.[1] Despite rapid economic growth, Ethiopia remains one of the world's poorest countries, with per capita GDP being US$472 as of 2012.

Since August 1995, Ethiopia has been structured into nine regional states and two city administration councils under a constitutional federal system. In addition to receiving federal subsidies, the regions are mandated to generate local revenue. Decentralization from the regional to the woreda (district) level was initiated in 2002 except in the emerging regions, in which decentralization started in 2004. Woredas are the basic decentralized administrative unit, and each has an administrative council composed of elected members. The country is highly heterogeneous, with large socioeconomic differences across regional states and across urban and rural areas. The decentralized levels receive block grants from the federal level based on a block grant formula.

Ethiopia's Growth and Transformation Plan (GTP) 2011–15 has a strong focus on the Millennium Development Goals (MDGs) and gives high priority to human development. In line with the objective of poverty eradication and social development, the government of Ethiopia (GOE) has invested in both physical and human capital formation to address the challenges of achieving the MDGs. Box 1.1 presents the health sector goal, objectives, and targets set under the GTP.

Box 1.1   Health Sector Goals, Objectives, and Targets Set under the Growth and Transformation Plan

Goal: Improve the health of the population through provision of promotive, preventive, curative, and rehabilitative health services by focusing on the following two objectives:

Improve access to health service: This objective includes availing of affordable health service to improve the health of mothers, neonates, children, adolescents, and youth; reducing the incidence and prevalence of communicable and noncommunicable diseases; and improving hygiene and environmental health.

Improve quality of health services: This objective includes provision of health services according to standards set for health facilities at all levels.

In terms of specific health outcomes, the GTP has the following goals:

- Decrease maternal mortality ratio
- Decrease under-five mortality
- Increase use of family planning services
- Increase Pentavalent 3 immunization coverage
- Reduce incidence of human immunodeficiency virus (HIV) in adults
  Reduce prevalence of malaria

Source: MOFED 2010.

Health Sector Development Programs Overview

The National Health Policy gives strong emphasis to fulfilling the needs of less privileged rural communities, which constitute about 83 percent of the total population. Health Sector Development Program (HSDP) is a mechanism translating the country's health policies into actions (Federal Ministry of Health [FMOH] 2010c). It covers the period from 1997/98 to 2014/15 through consecutive multiyear plans. The HSDP is a key GTP component, and an important vehicle for achieving GTP targets for building human capital.

The currently implemented HSDP IV (2010/11–2014/15) is part of the government's overall vision for Ethiopia to become a middle-income country soon after the MDG target date of 2015. GOE's commitment to achieving universal health coverage (UHC) is clearly reflected in HSDP IV. To achieve this objective, "the health sector of Ethiopia will have to stretch to attain its objectives of reaching every section of the population with effective health interventions." The scope of HSDP IV covers the entire health sector in Ethiopia and includes all sources of financing and engages all stakeholders.

HSDP IV envisages addressing key gaps in health systems to deliver essential health services and improve coverage for evidence-based interventions, with attention to quality and to reducing inequities. Specific strategies include (1) expanding the HEP to urban and pastoralist communities and improving quality in the rural areas; (2) putting in place a comprehensive, continuous quality improvement system; (3) scaling up of civil service reform to enhance leadership at all levels of the system and build implementation capacities; (4) giving special attention to programs that did not achieve their targets; (5) developing human resources and motivational strategies to address the gaps in availability and skill mix; (6) developing health infrastructure with focus on enabling selected health centers to provide emergency surgical and comprehensive emergency obstetric care, logistic hubs for effective storage, distribution of pharmaceuticals, and information and communication technology infrastructure; (7) giving special attention to four regions facing unique challenges in service delivery and health systems development; (8) raising community awareness and training health professionals in health effects of climate change, working in collaboration with the Environmental Protection Agency; and (9) gender mainstreaming to increase the use of health services by women.

The Annual Review Meeting (ARM) of HSDP is organized each year to review the progress made in implementing and addressing challenges. Participants of the ARM are key stakeholders of the health sector, including representatives from FMOH, regional health bureaus, woreda health bureaus, nongovernmental organizations (NGOs), academia, and development partners. During each ARM, annual health sector performance reports for the past year and annual woreda-based plans for the next year are presented and discussed.

Institutional Arrangements for HSDP IV

Ethiopia follows a decentralized federal structure of administration. The Constitution stipulates shared responsibilities for health policy making, regulation, and service delivery between the FMOH, regional health bureaus (RHBs), and woreda health offices (WorHOs). Proclamation No. 475/1995 of the Federal Democratic Republic of Ethiopia defines the powers and duties of executive agencies.

- The role of FMOH includes several aspects: (1) the FMOH is in charge of national health formulation, strategic and annual planning, resource mobilization, donor coordination, and monitoring and evaluation. Appropriate platforms are established for mutual accountability, information flow, and efficient use of resources; (2) the FMOH provides support to expand service delivery. It has directorates responsible for coordinating and supporting the Health Extension Program. It is also in charge of establishment and operation of national referral hospitals and national-level study and research centers; (3) the FMOH determines standards and operational protocols, regulation of health services, and professional education related to health. The Medical Service Directorate coordinates development of standards for curative care and monitors their compliance by hospitals and health centers. The Food, Medicine and Health Care Administration and Control Authority (FMHACA)[2] is responsible for safety and quality of foods and medicines;

licensing and inspection of health professionals, pharmaceuticals, food establishments, and health institutions; and (4) the Pharmaceutical Fund and Supply Agency[3] (PFSA) is responsible for procurement and distribution of safe and affordable essential medicines, and medical supplies and equipment, including supplies for priority national programs and the operation of the drug revolving fund.

- Role of RHBs: The nine regional health bureaus and two city administrations are responsible for plans and programs in their respective areas to deliver health services based on the national health policy, for health service delivery within the region (including all types of hospitals), for licensing of health facilities, and ensuring an adequate supply of safe and affordable medicines and supplies. RHBs provide technical support to WorHOs.
- Role of WorHOs: WorHOs fall under the administrative control of Woreda Councils; they manage and coordinate the primary health care units (health centers and health posts), and are responsible for planning, financing, and monitoring health progress and service delivery within the woreda (FMOH 2010).

There are well-established governance structures at different levels of the Ethiopian health sector as shown in figure 1.1. The Joint Consultative Forum (JCF) chaired by the minister of health and co-chaired by the lead partner in the sector is the highest body for dialogue on sector policy and reform issues between the government of Ethiopia (GOE), its partners, and wider stakeholders. The JCF also oversees the allocation, implementation, and use of the MDG Performance Fund, PBS, Global Alliance for Vaccines and Immunization (GAVI), and other

Figure 1.1   Governance Arrangements for HSDP IV

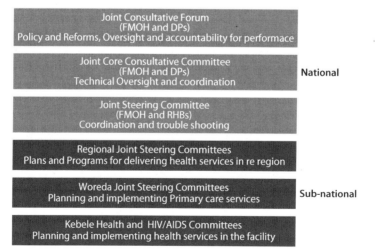

Source: World Bank 2012b.
Note: FMOH = Federal Ministry of Health; RHB = Regional Health Bureau; AIDS = acquired immune deficiency syndrome; HIV = human immunodeficiency virus.

donor-supported projects ensuring effective linkages between support provided by different partners, regional bureaus, and other sectors.

The Joint Core Coordinating Committee (JCCC) is the technical arm for the JCF. It is chaired by the director general of Policy, Planning and Finance General Directorate. The JCCC provides operational oversight and monitors the implementation of all pooled and non-pooled funds provided by partners to the health sector. The JCCC is also responsible for organizing and coordinating monitoring and evaluation of the program, as well as facilitating relevant meetings and missions, including technical assignments recommended by JCF. The regional health bureaus are engaged through the FMOH-RHB Joint Steering Committee. The program-based technical working groups focus on addressing specific technical issues in priority national programs.

Regions, zones, and woredas, respectively, are expected to establish joint steering committees, which meet quarterly to discuss and address implementation bottlenecks. Each kebele (village) is expected to have a committee on health and human immunodeficiency virus (HIV)/acquired immune deficiency syndrome (AIDS) that meets once every month. Most regions have established governing boards for health centers and hospitals that include representatives of the community. These boards meet once every quarter to discuss and endorse plans as well as to monitor performance.

Service Delivery System

Ethiopia uses a three-tier public health system (figure 1.2) to deliver essential health services and ensure referral linkages. At primary-care level, a primary care unit is composed of primary hospital, health center, and health post. The secondary level comprises general hospitals. A general hospital provides inpatient and ambulatory services and serves as a referral center for primary hospitals. The tertiary-care level comprises specialized hospitals and serves as a referral from general hospitals.

This health service delivery system corresponds to the administrative structure of the government. Tertiary providers are financed and managed by the federal-level health authority, that is, FMOH; secondary hospitals, mostly regional hospitals, are financed and managed by the regional-level health authority, that is, RHBs; and the primary-level providers are financed and managed by the woreda-level health authority, that is, WorHO. Within the woreda level, there are three level of providers: primary hospitals, approximately one planned for each woreda,[4] serve about 60,000–100,000 people; health centers, one planned for 40,000 people in urban areas and for 15,000–25,000 people in rural areas; and health posts, one planned for 3,000–5,000 people. Hospitals and health centers are staffed by conventional health professionals such as physicians, nurses, and midwives. As part of an innovative human resource initiative, health officers are also trained and deployed to hospitals and health centers, and serve similar functions as physicians. Health posts are expected to be staffed by health extension workers, who will be described in greater detail in later sections.

Figure 1.2   Structure of Ethiopia's Three-Tier Public Health System

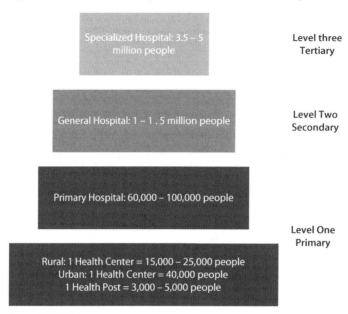

Source: FMOH 2010c.

The public sector remains an important source for health care and the major recipient of health sector resources. Private providers (for-profit and nonprofit) received only 16 percent of total national expenditure on health. HSDP IV envisaged that public–private partnerships would be enhanced through collaborative endeavors on selected health sector priority programs and health system issues. Areas identified for such collaboration include expansion of health infrastructure, local production of pharmaceuticals, provision of health services, training of health professionals, mobilization of resources for the health sector, and partnerships with professional associations on improving quality of health services and reducing professional malpractice.

Health Financing System

HSDP IV used the marginal budgeting for bottlenecks tool to estimate resource needs for achieving MDGs. The baseline scenario envisages using existing infrastructure and human resources to provide universal access to health centers with a backup of primary hospitals providing emergency surgical and obstetric care. The best-case scenario envisages providing effective clinical care at all levels of the health system. It is estimated that the total budget required will be US$8.8 billion and US$10.8 billion, respectively, for the baseline and best-case scenarios (FMOH 2010).

Currently in Ethiopia, there are three main types of funding sources for the health sector: general government revenue, development partners, and households. Funds from these sources flow to facilities through different pathways. Figure 1.3 outlines the flow of funds from different sources.

Figure 1.3 HSDP IV Financing Sources and Funds Flow

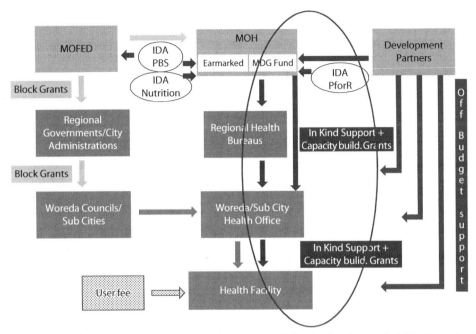

Note: MOFED = Ministry of Finance and Economic Development; MDG = Millennium Development Goal; IDA = International Development Association; PBS = Promotion of Basic Services; MOH = Ministry of Health.

Funds from GOE revenue flow to the health sector through the treasury system. At federal level the Ministry of Finance and Economic Development (MOFED) transfers funds to federal-level agencies (for example, Ministry of Health) in line items and to regional bureaus of finance and economic development (BOFEDs) in block grants. At regional level, BOFEDs transfer funds to regional-level agencies (for example, regional health bureaus) in line items, and to woreda offices of finance and economic development (WOFEDs) in block grants. At woreda level, WOFEDS allocate funds to facilities/workers in line items, mostly salaries due to limited funds. The fiscal transfers from the federal government to the regions are based on three criteria: population, revenue-generating capacity, and development status. Many regions have been implementing a similar formula to transfer funds down to the woredas based on current expenditures, development status, and revenue-generating capacity.

Funds from development partners flow in four ways: (1) channeled to MOFED and allocated to regions/woredas together with funds from government revenues, for example, the Promotion of Basic Services Program[5] that started in 2006; (2) channeled to the nonearmarked MDG Performance Fund (MDGPF)[6] and allocated to health facilities through in-kind transfer and capacity-building grants; (3) channeled to Federal Ministry of Health as program/project fund for specific purposes, agreed between FMOH and donors; (4) channeled to implementation partners chosen by donors based on the agreement between themselves. Some examples of this channel are the United States Agency for International Development (USAID), the President's Emergency Plan for AIDS Relief (PEPFAR), and the Centers for Disease Control and Prevention (CDC).

Funds from households flow to health facilities in the form of user fees. User fees are usually carried over from history, and therefore tend to be outdated and vary between facilities. Health facilities are required to post fee schedules in public areas.

The five rounds of National Health Accounts (NHA) reveal the level and mix of different financing sources over a period of 15 years (1995/96–2010/11). The percentage of total health expenditure out of GDP remains steadily around 4 percent. Per capita spending on health increased from US$4.5 to US$20.8 between 1995/96 and 2010/11, with substantial increases from all sources (figure 1.4). The composition of different sources shifted over time due to different rates of increase. External assistance became the primary source in 2004/05 and has reached about half of the total health expenditure as of 2010/11. Conversely, the proportion of GOE spending almost halved from 33.4 to 15.6 percent. From 1999/00 to 2010/11.

What is not reflected in figure 1.3 is the government's plan to provide financial protection through a combination of two health insurance schemes: (1) Social Health Insurance (SHI) Scheme among formal sector employees and their family members (approximately 11 percent of the population); and (2) Community-Based Health Insurance (CBHI) Scheme among informal sector employees and rural residents (approximately 89 percent of the population). The Ethiopian Health Insurance Agency (EHIA) is entrusted with the responsibility of administering both SHI and CBHI, and it is already in its formative stage.

Figure 1.4 Level of Health Expenditures over Time

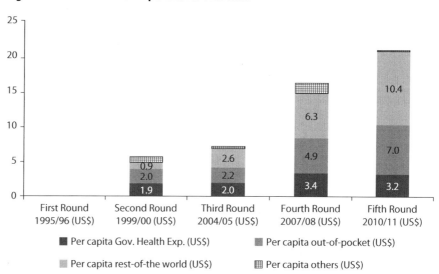

Sources: FMOH 2006, 2010, 2014.

Through these two schemes, GOE aims to cover about 17 percent of the population by 2015. The Parliament has already approved SHI proclamation, alongside the benefits package regulations. The launch time of the SHI will be subject to the final decision of the cabinet. CBHI has been piloted in 13 woredas and is currently scaling up to 172 woredas.

Targeted subsidies are allocated to cover CBHI contributions for indigents, accounting for about 10 percent of the population in each pilot woreda. The fee waiver screening and identification of eligible beneficiaries are conducted with community participation. The selected beneficiaries are given a certificate that entitles them to free health care services. The experience is diverse across regions, and a recent review of the health sector reform recommended further improvement in "the targeting and identification of the right beneficiaries." All public health facilities are expected to post a list of exempted services in the waiting area.

Notes

1. Ethiopia Economic Update, World Bank, September 2012.
2. FMHACA is one of the four agencies under the FMOH with specific mandates. The head of FMHACA is appointed by the prime minister and reports to both FMOH and the Ministry of Finance and Economic Development (MOFED).
3. Same as endnote 4.
4. Ethiopia is in the process of completing construction of all planned primary hospitals.
5. The first two phases of this program were called Protection of Basic Services.
6. The MDGPF pools' non-earmarked funds provided by partners supporting health sector. The specific scope of activities to be financed by MDGPF is determined through a consultative process involving all key stakeholders every year. The Joint Financing Arrangement (JFA) sets out the overarching governance and reporting requirements for the Fund. As of 2014, 11 partners channel resources to the MDGPF. They are Australian AID, UK Department for International Development (DFID), Spanish Development Cooperation, Italian Cooperation, Irish Aid, UNFPA, UNICEF, WHO, the Netherlands government, the World Bank, and the European Commission.

CHAPTER 2

Ethiopia Health Extension Program

Health Extension Program (HEP) is one of the strategies adopted in Ethiopia with a view to achieving universal coverage of primary health care among the rural population by 2009, in a context of limited resources. The overall goal of HEP is to create a healthy society and reduce maternal and child morbidity and mortality rates. The specific objectives are the following: (1) reduce morbidity and mortality of children and mothers; (2) reduce morbidity and mortality from HIV/AIDS, tuberculosis, and malaria through development of community skills and knowledge; (3) prevent diseases caused by malnutrition, poor personal hygiene, and contaminated food; (4) prevent accidents and emergency illnesses, and administer first aid to the injured and sick; and (5) develop community awareness, knowledge, and skills in rural Ethiopia to prevent contamination from common sources, including human excreta, animal wastes, and pesticides.

The HEP is a flagship program of the government of Ethiopia. It was launched by the Federal Ministry of Health in 2003 with the goal of improving health outcomes in Ethiopia by targeting households and communities. The program was originally launched in 2003 in the country's four big agrarian regions and has made important contributions to Ethiopia's achievements in the area of health. The HEP has been expanded to the remaining regions in the country and tailored to the particular requirements of the pastoral communities in 2006, and of urban areas in 2010.

This is a program that is deeply rooted in communities, providing primary-level preventive activities to household members. The program encourages families to be responsible for their own health by promoting knowledge dissemination and adoption of hygiene practice and feeding practice, and appropriate health-seeking behavior from professionals and proper community management. This community outreach ensures a sense of ownership and of sustainable changes in communities.

The HEP implementation manual states that health extension workers lead the planning, implementation, and evaluation of community outreach activities. Volunteer community health promoters (vCHPs), most of whom were organized into the health development army (HDA) later, are expected to apply the health education in their own households and help HEWs by mobilizing the community and by acting as community role models to form more model households. HEWs also leverage the support from traditional associations like Ekub and Edir and involve women and youth associations in communities.

In addition to community activities, HEP also provides health post-based basic services, including preventive health services such as immunizations and injectable contraceptives, and limited basic curative services such as first aid and treatment of malaria, intestinal parasites, and other ailments. Case referral to health centers is also provided when more complicated care is needed.

The services provided under HEP include 16 essential health packages under four major program areas:

- *Hygiene and environmental sanitation:* (1) proper and safe excreta disposal system, (2) proper and safe solid and liquid waste management, (3) water supply safety measures, (4) food hygiene and safety measures, (5) healthy home environment, (6) arthropods and rodent control, and (7) personal hygiene.
- *Disease prevention and control:* (1) HIV/AIDS prevention and control, (2) TB prevention and control, (3) malaria prevention and control, and (4) first aid.
- *Family health services:* (1) maternal and child health, (2) family planning, (3) immunization, (4) adolescent reproductive health, and (5) nutrition.
- *Health Education and Communication:* Cross cutting.

The HEP benefits from close collaboration with technical vocational education training (TVET) institutions under the Ministry of Education. The TVET institutions provide theoretical training for deployed HEWs. In addition, TVET institutions develop a health extension service occupational standard. In this standard, each distinct work activity is defined as a Unit of Competence, with detailed documentation in standard format about the following contents:

- *Occupational title and National TVET Qualification Framework (NTQF) level*
- *Unit title*
- *Unit code*
- *Unit descriptor*
- *Elements and performance criteria*
- *Variables and range statement*
- *Evidence guide*

Table 2.1 presents key elements of each activity required for health extension service NTQF level III, the starting level for the majority of HEWs. Appendix A also describes full contents for the activity of "Collect, Maintain, and Utilize Community Health Data" at this level.

Table 2.1 Health Extension Services Package

Service package	Description of key elements
1. Collect, maintain, and utilize community health	• Plan and prepare necessary materials for data collection • Collect data that need to be entered into the health database system • Collect vital events and surveillance data • Prepare and submit reports • Contribute to working with community to identify health needs
2. Perform community mobilization and provide health education	• Participate in the determination of community health information needs • Participate in the preparation of health information • Provide health promotion and education services • Train model families • Perform advocacy of identified health issues • Promote community mobilization on the identified health issues
3. Promote and implement hygiene and environmental health	• Promote and provide environmental and personal hygiene education • Establish and demonstrate community-appropriate sanitation technologies • Provide environmental health service
4. Prevent and control common communicable diseases	• Educate the community on early detection and prevention of communicable diseases • Perform disease surveillance • Follow up cases
5. Prevent and control common noncommunicable diseases	• Educate the community on healthy lifestyle and early detection of disease • Screen and refer clients requiring further investigation and management • Follow up cases and promote community-based rehabilitation
6. Promote community nutrition	• Collect appropriate information for preparing nutrition education • Provide basic nutrition information/ education to the clients • Monitor client response to the information/education
7. Promote and provide antenatal care	• Provide antenatal examination and information for pregnant women • Conduct home visit and refer pregnant women with health problems
8. Promote institutional delivery and provide delivery service	• Support women during childbirth • Provide normal delivery • Provide immediate neonatal care
9. Promote and provide postnatal care	• Provide services for lactating mothers on infant care, nutrition, and exclusive breastfeeding • Organize and follow up maternal health programs
10. Promote child survival, growth and development, and apply Integrated Community Case Management (ICCM)	• Promote child survival, and growth and development activities • Access and manage common childhood illness • Refer child requiring further care
11. Promote and implement immunization	• Plan immunization programs • Conduct immunization programs
12. Promote and provide family planning service	• Educate the community on family planning options • Educate adolescents on family planning and STIs
13. Promote and provide adolescent and youth reproductive health (RH)	• Plan adolescent and youth RH services; promote adolescent and youth RH services • Provide RH service package • Register and document RH records

table continues next page

Table 2.1 Health Extension Services Package *(continued)*

Service package	Description of key elements
14. Provide first aid	• Assess and identify client's condition • Provide first aid service • Refer client requiring further care
15. Manage community health service	• Follow organizational guidelines, understand health policy and service delivery system • Work ethically • Provide team leadership and assign responsibilities • Establish quality standards, assess and record quality of service delivery • Manage work and resources at a health post • Lead workplace communication
16. Respond to emergencies	• Prepare for emergency situations; evaluate the emergency • Act in an emergency • Apply essential first aid techniques

Source: Ethiopia Federal Ministry of Education 2014.

Context

The Health Extension Program was developed with full recognition of the macro resource constraints Ethiopia faces. It was developed in a context where health outcomes and coverage of essential services were very poor, and where there was a large disparity between rural and urban populations, and between better-educated and less-educated people (table 2.2 and table 2.3). Motivations for developing the HEP include the following:

- Low coverage for health interventions known to have high impact. For example, in 2005 only 1.3 percent of under-five children slept under insecticide-treated mosquito nets; 32 percent of children exclusively breastfed; 37 percent of children with diarrhea were given oral rehydration therapy; 17 percent of children with a fever or cough were brought to a health facility; immunization coverage remained low; and only 6 percent of mothers were assisted by a skilled health worker during delivery (CSA and ICF International 2012).
- Low access to essential health services, particularly for the rural poor, and an overall shortage of health workers.
- A critical shortage of skilled health workers. Although Ethiopia has one of the highest numbers of health workers in Sub-Saharan Africa, its large population leaves it with a very low health worker-to-population ratio. The Federal Ministry of Health reported 65,554 health workers—public, private, and NGO—which translates into a total density of 0.84 health worker per 1,000 population (Feysa et al. 2012).
- Weak institutional synergies that limited the expansion of primary health care services.

Table 2.2 Status of Health Outcomes in Ethiopia before HEP

Background characteristic	Total fertility rate	Height-for-age	Weight-for-height	Weight-for-age	Infant mortality $(_1q_0)$*	Child mortality $(_4q_1)$**	Under-five mortality $(_5q_0)$***
Residence							
Urban	3.3	42.3	5.5	33.7	96.5	57.6	148.6
Rural	6.4	52.6	11.1	48.7	114.7	87.8	192.5
Education							
No education	6.2	52.9	11.4	49.6	119.1	89.0	197.4
Primary	5.1	49.1	8.8	40.4	85.0	67.9	147.1
Secondary and higher	3.1	32.9	6.7	27.7	63.5	27.4	89.2
Total	5.9	51.5	10.5	47.2	112.9	84.5	187.8

Source: Ethiopia Central Statistical Authority (CSA) 2011.
Note: *Infant mortality $(_1q_0)$ = The probability of dying before the first birthday; **Child mortality $(_4q_1)$ = The probability of dying between the first and the fifth birthday; ***Under-five mortality $(_5q_0)$ = The probability of dying between birth and the fifth birthday.

Table 2.3 Status of Basic Service Delivery in Ethiopia before HEP

Background characteristic	Antenatal care	Skilled birth attendance	DPT3
Residence			
Urban	66.6	34.5	51.3
Rural	21.6	2.3	17.2
Education			
No education	21.0	2.5	15.8
Primary	45.0	10.4	35.0
Secondary and higher	71.7	45.0	53.8
Total	26.7	5.6	20.7

Source: Ethiopia Central Statistical Authority 2011.
Note: DPT3 = Diphtheria, pertussis, and tetanus immunization coverage.

The HEP, initiated and led by GOE, was designed on the basis of experiences and challenges in the earlier community health workers' initiatives, such as those involving traditional birth attendants and other voluntary workers. In addition, there has been South-South cooperation and experience-sharing with Kerala State, India.

Key Actors

As key vehicles for the implementation of the HEP, HEWs were deployed to kebeles (villages); model families were trained in communities; and the health development army was mobilized. Together, they form key forces for the implementation of the HEP.

Health Extension Workers

The HEWs are the key drivers of the program. Two HEWs are deployed for each health post serving 3,000–5,000 population. They are recruited based on nationally agreed criteria that include residence in the village, capacity to speak local language, graduation from 10th grade, and willingness to remain in the village and serve communities. Selection is done by a committee comprising members nominated by the local community and representatives from the woreda (district) health office, the woreda capacity-building office, and the woreda education office.

All selected HEWs go through a year-long training, which includes both theoretical training in training institutions and practical training in health centers. The theoretical training is provided in technical vocational education centers under the Ministry of Education. Upon graduation, HEWs are assigned to their home villages to provide HEP health services. The village council and the health center support the HEWs. Training in providing community-based care, such as treatment of sick children and conduct of clean and safe deliveries, and some refresher courses are also provided to some HEWs.

Once deployed to their respective communities, HEWs divide their time between providing services at health posts and undertaking community promotion programs at household level. At health posts, HEWs spend a certain percentage of their time (25 percent at the initial stage of the program and 50 percent currently) providing services that include immunizations, injectable contraception, and limited basic curative services such as provision of anti-malaria treatment, first aid, and management of diarrheal diseases and intestinal parasites. The community promotion program is centered on health development army teams who are under the supervision and guidance of the HEWs. During the domiciliary care, HEWs and development army teams provide support to households for behavioral change and motivate them to utilize primary health care services. Along with the volunteer community promoters, HEWs are also responsible for training model families—as described below.

HEWs receive supervisory support from upper administrative levels as part of the sectors' integrated supervision system. A supervisory team consisting of members from different disciplines was established at the federal, regional, and woreda levels to provide guidance and support. The teams are involved in all aspects of program management, including planning, implementation, and monitoring and evaluation. Members of the team are trained in skills needed for supportive supervision (facilitation, interpersonal communication, problem solving, and analytical skills); oriented to various tools and methods (such as peer review and performance assessment tools); and provided with opportunities to frequently upgrade their technical skills. The supervisors are trained in a specially designed curriculum. At each level, the supervisory team prepares its own annual plan, checklists, and detailed schedule for each supervisory visit. A typical supervision in a region cascades from regional level down to woreda, health center, and health posts. Supervisory teams also actively engage regional and woreda councils, as well as kebele administrations, particularly for issues that go beyond the health sector itself.

Model Families

Model Families: Model families are those households that are (1) trained in maternal health, malaria prevention and control, and hygiene and environmental sanitation packages; (2) able to implement these packages after the training; and (3) able to influence their relatives and neighbors to adopt the same practices. Before the introduction of the health development army, model families were expected to gather regularly for experience-sharing. They now work as part of the army to engage communities for health improvement.

Candidates during the early phase of model family training include households with models in the agricultural extension program, traditional birth attendants, volunteer community health workers, or health focal persons in the kebele, because it is believed they are ready for change and can also influence the behavior and practice of community members.

When implementing the training, priority is given to activities that are easy and inexpensive to implement, and are not contradictory to the community's values. This strategy ensures acceptability by the community and facilitates the scale-up of changes in the community. The contents of the model family package are presented in box 2.1.

Box 2.1   Packages Included for Model Family Training

Packages included for Model Family Training

- Maintaining personal hygiene
- Building and using latrines
- Storing and using clean potable water
- ANC, delivery, and postnatal care services
- Immunization services
- Breastfeeding and complementary feeding
- Family planning service
- Pregnant and lactating women feeding
- Infant care
- Malaria prevention and control
- HIV/AIDS prevention and control
- Food and environmental sanitation
- Home sanitation and waste disposal
- Solid and liquid waste management/disposal
- Prevention and control of flies and insects
- Preparation and feeding of nutritional foods

---

box continues next page

Box 2.1   Packages Included for Model Family Training *(continued)*

- Supplementary food for children
- Treatment of sick child at home/health facility
- Youth reproductive health and premarital HIV testing
- TB prevention and control
- Benefits of first aid treatment
- Identification and prevention of epidemics
- Female genital mutilation
- Uvulectomy
- Milk tooth extraction
- Blood letting
- Early marriage

Source: FMOH 2012b.

To graduate as model families, households who have undergone model family training are evaluated for their work and changes in their own practices within six months after completion of training. Box 2.2 presents indicators used for evaluating whether households should be graduated as model families. People from the neighboring community are invited to graduation to observe the honor, to help expand the program in neighboring areas.

Box 2.2   Model Family Graduation Criteria

Maternal and child health

- Fully vaccinated children (one-year old)
- Monthly growth monitoring for children age 0–2
- Contraceptive use for women in reproductive age
- Women received antenatal care for their pregnancy
- Women gave birth in facilities/ assisted by skilled professionals
- Women received postnatal care
- Exclusive breast feeding

Malaria prevention and control

- Proper and continuous usage of ITN (insecticide-treated mosquito nets)
- Participation of the family in the social mobilization campaign on malaria control activities such as environmental management activities
- Walls and roofs are not painted for six months after insecticide is sprayed

box continues next page

Box 2.2 Model Family Graduation Criteria (continued)

Hygiene and environmental sanitation

- Availability, maintenance, and continuous use of latrine
- Personal hygiene practice
- Healthy housing
- Cleanliness of the residence and surrounding areas
- Separate food preparation area
- Separate animal shed away from family living rooms

Source: FMOH 2012b.

Health Development Army

Health Development Army: HDA refers to an organized movement of communities forged through participatory learning and action meetings. The HDA is designed to improve the implementation capacity of the health sector by engaging communities to identify local challenges and corresponding strategies. It is also designed for scaling up best practices from one part of the country to another.

The government of Ethiopia prioritizes the establishment of a functional HDA. The HDA is regarded as a key vehicle that would help Ethiopia achieve its ambitious Health Sector Development Program (HSDP) targets. A coordinating body at each level of the system has been established to monitor the implementation of HDA. The members of the coordinating body are drawn from relevant sectors such as agriculture, education, water, women's affairs, and social protection (FMOH 2012b). The coordinating body is chaired by the administrator or deputy administrator, and the health sector serves as the secretary. The coordinating body meets regularly to review the performance of the HDA with special emphasis on maternal and newborn health outcomes. Furthermore, this body is mandated to set up teams that conduct onsite data verification once every quarter.

A functional HDA requires the establishment of health development teams that comprise up to 30 households residing in the same neighborhood. The health development team is further divided into smaller groups of six members, commonly referred to as one-to-five networks. Leaders of the health development teams and the one-to-five networks are selected by their team members. The main criteria for selection of leaders include belonging to a model family, having the trust of members, and being able to mobilize the community. Specific responsibilities of the HDA team leaders include the following:

- Establish a one-to-five network and monitor the implementation of the HDA plan
- Be role models for others

- Gather status report on the one-to-five networks every two weeks. Analyze the data and identify the bottlenecks and the way forward, and share best experiences among the network members as well as with others.
- Mobilize communities for health activities and influence their own communities through the accelerated development strategy, which includes supporting families in terms of knowledge, and material and implementation capacity to bring about sustainable behavioral changes for improved health outcomes

The formation of the health development teams and the one-to-five networks is facilitated by HCs, HEWs and the kebele administration. A women-centered HDA approach was initially piloted in Tigray region, and then scaled up in all regions. The HDA one-to-five networks meet every week, and the HDA team leaders meet every two weeks.

Once groups are formed through participatory engagement of the community, leaders will go through an intensive training program that takes 15 days on average. The training emphasizes improving utilization of high-impact maternal and newborn health services. In a kebele of 1,000 households, on average 150 leaders are expected to go through the training program. The training is facilitated by HEWs with support from primary health care (PHC) units and woreda health offices. The HDA is designed to accomplish the following critical tasks:

- Identify salient bottlenecks at the local level that hinder families from utilizing key services and implementing the HEP, and prioritize the ones that must be addressed as a team
- Come up with feasible strategies to address these problems
- Implement the strategies
- Evaluate their own activities

The HDA also involves larger community meetings where all residents in a kebele will participate. These larger public conferences provide a platform to discuss prioritized bottlenecks and strategies, and to share best practices. These meetings are often led by the kebele administrator with support from HEWs.

In most of the regions, the leaders have gone through intensive training programs and have had to identify bottlenecks that hamper the implementation of HEP in their villages. During problem identification, emphasis was placed on cultural and attitude-related bottlenecks. The models were also engaged in identifying challenges in acquiring skills and supplies to implement interventions of the HEP. After they completed the training, leaders were encouraged to work with their team members in identifying attitude, skill, and supply bottlenecks; prioritize problems; and come up with strategies to address the problems. The strategies must be captured in a plan, and specific tasks assigned to team members. Leaders are also expected to identify group actions and include them in the plan.

The health development team meets to review their performance against the plan and evaluate each other every two weeks. They give grades, A, B, and C, for top, middle, and poor performers, respectively, on a monthly basis. A performance report including the grades has to be collated at the health development team level and sent to the HEWs.

Financing

HEP is mainly financed by two sources: the government and communities. GOE finances the program by covering salaries of all HEWs, and is responsible for management and supervision of the program. Communities' financial contribution to the program is often not in monetary form, but in in-kind contribution such as labor, food, and accommodation.

One significant element of the HEP cost is salaries for HEWs. Based on the information of average salary for HEWs, it is estimated that the payroll bill for 35,000 HEWs is around Br 630.0 million, equivalent to US$31.7 million. In other words, the cost of HEWs is Br 7.5 or US$0.38 per capita.[1] Comparison of the payroll bill for HEWs with overall government health expenditure[2] shows that the salary payment for HEWs accounts for 21 percent of recurrent expenditures, and 32 percent of the woreda-level recurrent expenditure. This is certainly not uniformly the case for all woredas. Figure 2.1 presents the distribution of HEW expenditures as a proportion of woreda recurrent health expenditures.[3] Most woredas spent between 20 and 40 percent on HEW expenditures.

Figure 2.1 Proportion of HEW Expenditures Out of Woreda Recurrent Expenditures in 2010/11

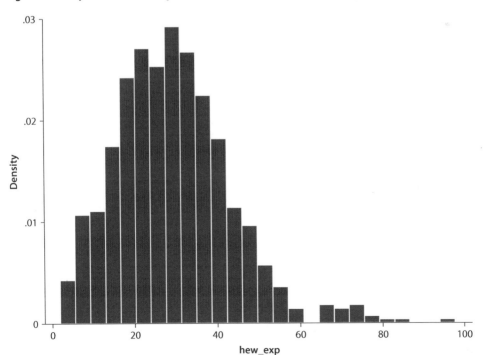

Source: MOFED account data.

Training model families and mobilization of HDA also require significant resources, but there is a lack of data on the cost for such activities. HEWs were surveyed to estimate average total cost incurred by a household to become a model family: the overall mean cost to become model families for those kebeles was Br 871. This translates to Br 10.8 billion or US$568 million for the 12 million model families that have been trained.

Notes

1. The monthly salary is assumed to be Br 1,500. This is based on data from the FMOH that specify the average monthly salary for a level IV HEW is Br 1,472. Per capita cost estimation uses the population size of 84 million. Exchange rate used is US$1 equivalent to Br 19.

2. 2010/11 government health expenditure data are used.

3. Woreda-level recurrent health expenditure is collected by the Poverty and Social Impact Analysis team under the PBS project. Estimated HEW expenditure is based on average HEW salary, the number of HEWs per 1,000 population at regional level, and population number at woreda level.

CHAPTER 3

Health Extension Program and Progress toward UHC

This section starts with the objective of this case study, which aims to examine how the Health Extension Program (HEP) has contributed to the country's progress toward Universal Health Coverage (UHC). A general framework on social determinants of health is then described, laying a motivating foundation for the conceptual model of HEP and UHC. Methodology and data are described following the conceptual model.

Objectives

As a low-income country, Ethiopia has made impressive progress in improving health outcomes with limited resources. The Interagency Group for Child Mortality Estimation reported that Ethiopia has achieved Millennium Development Goal (MDG) 4, three years ahead of target, with under-five mortality at 68 per 1,000 live births in 2012.

Since the HEP was introduced as a strategy to move toward UHC in Ethiopia, this study aims to examine the following:

- How HEP has contributed to the country's progress toward UHC
- How other countries may learn from Ethiopia's experiences of HEP when designing their path toward UHC

A General Conceptual Framework on Social Determinants of Health

A conceptual framework for Social Determinants of Health developed by WHO's Commission on Social Determinants of Health (CSDH) identifies the social determinants of health and the social determinants of inequities in health; demonstrates how they relate to each other; and clarifies the mechanisms by which these determinants affect health and generate health inequities. The framework shows how social, economic, and political mechanisms give rise to a set of socioeconomic positions, whereby populations are stratified according to income, education, occupation, gender, race/ethnicity, and other factors. These socioeconomic positions in turn shape specific determinants of health status (intermediary determinants); based on their respective social status, individuals experience differences in exposure and vulnerability to health-compromising conditions, and thus, have different health outcomes. This implies that policies have to address both the level and the distribution of intermediary determinants to make an impact on health outcomes and health inequality. Figure 3.1 gives a graphical summary of the conceptual framework, and the paragraphs below describe the framework in detail.

The first element of the CSDH framework is socioeconomic and political context, which is a deliberately broad term that refers to the spectrum of factors in society that cannot be directly measured at the individual level. "Context" is a broad term that refers to a set of structural, cultural, and functional aspects of a social system that exert a powerful formative influence on patterns of social stratification and, thus, on people's health opportunities. In general, the mapping of context includes at least six points: (1) governance in the broadest sense and its processes, including definition of needs, patterns of discrimination, civil society participation, and accountability/transparence in public administration; (2) macroeconomic policy, including fiscal, monetary, balance of payments, and trade policies and underlying labor market structures; (3) social policies affecting factors such as labor, social welfare, land, and housing distribution; (4) public policy in other relevant areas such as education, medical care, water, and sanitation; (5) culture and societal values; and (6) epidemiological conditions, particularly in the case of major epidemics such as human immunodeficiency virus

Figure 3.1 Conceptual Framework on Social Determinants of Health

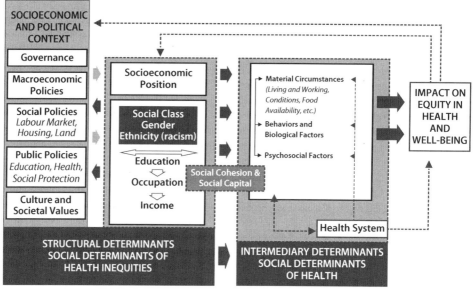

Source: Solar and Irwin 2010.

(HIV)/acquired immune deficiency syndrome (AIDS), which exert a powerful influence on social structures and must be factored into global and national policy setting.

The second element of the framework is socioeconomic position. Within each society, material and other resources are unequally distributed between individuals, which can be portrayed as a system of social stratification or social hierarchy. People attain different positions in the social hierarchy according mainly to their social class, occupational status, educational achievement, and income level. Their position in the social stratification system can be summarized as their socioeconomic position. The major variables used to operationalize the socioeconomic position include social stratification variables like income, education and occupation, social class, gender, and ethnicity.

The third element of the framework is intermediary determinants that are linked to a set of individual-level influences, including health-related behaviors and physiological factors. The intermediary factors flow from the configuration of underlying social stratification and, in turn, determine differences in exposure and vulnerability to health-compromising conditions. The main categories of intermediary determinants of health are material circumstances, psychosocial circumstances, and behavioral and/or biological factors.

- Material circumstances include determinants linked to the physical environment, such as housing (relating to both the dwelling itself and its location); consumption potential, that is, the financial means to buy healthy food, warm clothing, etc.; and the physical working and neighborhood environments. Depending on their quality, these circumstances provide resources for health and as well contain health risks. Differences in material living standards are probably the most important intermediary factor. The material standards of living tend to be more directly significant for the health status of marginalized groups and those with lower socioeconomic positions, especially if environmental factors are included. For example, housing characteristics measure material aspects of socioeconomic circumstances. Lack of running water and proper sanitation facilities will cause spread of waterborne communicable diseases. Incidence of malaria rises if a house is found in a neighborhood with stale water, without indoor spraying, and without use of mosquito nets.
- Social-environmental or psychosocial circumstances include psychosocial stressors (for example, negative life events and job strain), stressful living circumstances (for example, high debt), and lack of social support, coping styles, etc. Different social groups are exposed in different degrees to experiences and life situations that are perceived as threatening, frightening, and difficult for coping with in the everyday. This partly explains the long-term pattern of social inequalities in health. For example, high fertility is likely to be found in a society with a religion or culture against or ignorant of modern family planning methods.

• Behavioral and biological factors include smoking, diet, alcohol consumption, and lack of physical exercise, which again can be either health protecting and enhancing (like exercise) or health damaging (cigarette smoking and obesity); in between biological factors we include genetics factors, also from the perspective of social determinants of health, age, and sex distribution. Social inequalities in health have also been associated with social differences in lifestyle or behaviors. Such differences are found in nutrition, physical activity, and tobacco and alcohol consumption. Feeding practice is an important factor influencing children's nutritional status in developing countries, including exclusive breastfeeding for under-six-month olds and proper supplementary food for older babies.

Health system, a direct result of policy decisions made by governments, is posited as an intermediary social determinant of health in this model. Health system contributes to determining level of and inequality in health between different socioeconomic groups by addressing differences in exposure and vulnerability to health-compromising conditions and mediating their differences in the consequences for people's health and their social and economic circumstances.

This model highlights the distinction between determinants of health and the structural determinants of health inequities that shape the distribution of the determinants of health. Structural determinants of health inequities are structural social stratification mechanisms influenced by institutions and processes embedded in the socioeconomic and political context. Over the last 30 years, both improvements in health and health determinants have been observed in many countries; however, the link between disadvantaged socioeconomic positions and poor health is still not broken. This suggests that to reduce inequality in health, social, economic, and health policies must rebalance the distribution of health determining factors that are predetermined by structural determinants.

HEP and UHC Model Based on the General Framework

The general social determinants framework may be used to review how HEP has contributed to the country's move toward UHC. The HEP enters into this framework as part of the health system. UHC is reflected in this framework through the following aspects: (1) creation of a healthy society measured by intermediary determinants: circumstance factors, socioeconomic and psychological factors, and behavioral and biological factors; (2) improvement in coverage of services that minimize effects of life events; and (3) level and inequality of health outcomes.

As part of the health system, HEP is an intervention that promotes the move toward UHC by addressing all three elements of the framework. This specific HEP-UHC model is summarized in figure 3.2.

Figure 3.2 Health Extension Program and Universal Health Coverage Model in Ethiopia

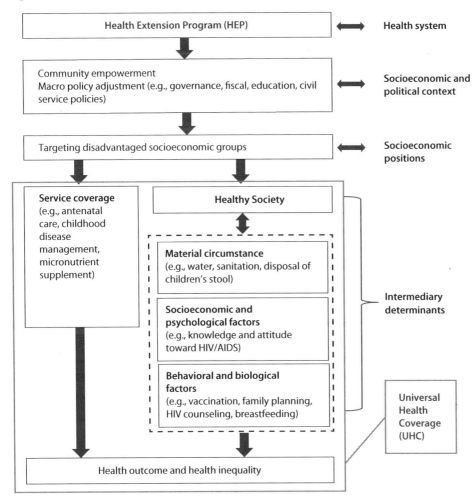

Source: Authors' generation.
Note: AIDS = acquired immune deficiency syndrome; HIV = human immunodeficiency virus.

First element, socioeconomic and political context:

- The HEP empowers communities by training model families who will further influence their communities, by advocating community participation and piloting innovative activities that in turn change the socioeconomic and political context influencing social stratification.
- The HEP is an innovative transformation to the country health system, and a number of policies have been put in place to ensure its implementation:
  o Governance: the design and implementation of HEP has been driven by a strong political commitment and has been guided by extensive consultation with key stakeholders.

o Fiscal policy: HEWs are recruited as civil servants and put on the payroll formally. Their salaries are paid by woredas from block grants transferred from MOFED via regions. The Ministry of Health uses resources from the MDG Performance Fund to provide in-kind transfers to ensure drugs and commodities are available to HEWs.

o Education: The Ministry of Health has undertaken the training for health extension workers through their technical and vocational training institutions, and developed occupational standards for each level of the health extension service.

o Health human resource policy: HEWs are testimony to the country's flexibility in developing the health human resource workforce, with relatively shorter training periods and lower entry bars. There are discussions about setting policies on how HEWs can enter the regular career ladder, for example, by becoming nurses or health officers after enhanced training. GOE is also in the process of upgrading health extension workers to the next level once they fulfill specified requirements.

Second element, socioeconomic positions:

• The HEP targets disadvantaged socioeconomic groups by having health extension workers and the health development army work in their own communities, identifying bottlenecks that compromise health conditions of disadvantaged groups, and providing free services at community level.

Third element, intermediary factors:

• The HEP decreases populations' exposure and vulnerability to health compromising factors, as follows:

o By improving their material circumstances, for example, through construction of latrines, waste management, and distribution of bed nets.

o By improving their socio-environmental and psychological circumstances. For example, HEWs educate communities about HIV/AIDS—one graduation criterion for model families is "having knowledge about HIV/AIDS with no stigma and discrimination toward those living with HIV/AIDS."

o By adjusting their behavioral and biological factors, for example, through training in personal hygiene, education in nutrition, home care of sick children, child growth monitoring, immunization, basic maternal health, and family planning.

• The HEP provides services at health posts to minimize consequence of diseases or life events on health (for example, treatment of fever, case referral, antenatal care, clean delivery, and postnatal care).

Methods

A quantitative analysis is undertaken to understand how the HEP has enabled progress toward UHC; lessons for other countries are based on existing literature. This section focuses on the methods of the quantitative analysis.

It is not feasible to conduct an ideal impact evaluation on the impact of HEP and UHC because the HEP was introduced at national level, and there was no academic impact evaluation put in place for a comparison with a counterfactual scenario. Considering data availability, this study therefore undertakes a pre-post type comparison of main indicators of interest. In the meantime, we choose a few proxy indicators to simulate the counterfactual situation as if there were no HEP.

The period from 2005 to 2011 was chosen for the following reasons: First, the two Ethiopia Demographic and Health Surveys (EDHSs) undertaken in 2005 and 2011 provide reliable data on intermediary factors (material circumstances, socioeconomic and psychological circumstances, behavioral and biological factors), and coverage of services and health outcomes; second, this comparison to a large extent reflects the situation before and after the introduction of HEP (introduced in 2003/04), as the period from 2004 to 2005 was mostly for implementation preparation. For a few indicators where data are available for 2014, comparison was made between 2005 and 2014, for example, coverage of antenatal care and modern contraceptives.

Based on the HEP and UHC model, the main indicators of interest are the intermediary factors and coverage of services. Chapter 3 describes specifics about the variables that operationalize these indicators.

We examine relative changes of the main indicators of interest during the study period (2005 to 2010/11). Taking indicator X as an example, the following formula is used to calculate its relative change, where X_{2011} denotes the level of X in 2011; X_{2005} denotes the level of X in 2005.

$$\text{relative change of } X = \frac{X_{2011} - X_{2005}}{X_{2005}}$$

In addition to relative change at national level, we compare relative changes between different socioeconomic groups, that is, groups by residence, education group, and wealth status,[1] as equity can only be improved when the outcome variables change at a faster pace for disadvantaged people than for better-off people. For example, the HEP may be considered pro-poor if outcome variables for poor people changed faster than for non-poor people.

We also use the movement of concentration curves to examine whether there is any reduction in inequality. The concentration curve plots the cumulative percentage of the variable of interests (y-axis) against the cumulative percentage of the population (x-axis), ranked by wealth status, beginning with the poorest and ending with the richest. A diagonal line is always presented with concentration curves to show the ideal situation where coverage of services is the same across all groups. The distance between the diagonal line and a concentration curve shows the extent of inequality: the larger the distance, the more inequitable the coverage of services. Group-level data (the mean for each wealth quintile) is used to plot concentration curves in this study.

Data

The main indicators of interests include (1) HEP direct outputs, (2) material circumstances, (3) socioeconomic and psychological circumstances, (4) behavioral and biological factors, and (5) coverage of services minimizing consequences of disease and life events.

Table 3.1 presents the main indicators of interest under each type of concept as well as proxy indicators for a counterfactual situation.

Table 3.1 Variable Overview

Concepts	Variable
HEP outputs	• Number of HEWs deployed • Number of model families trained and graduated • Number of HDA mobilized • Number of latrines constructed • Number of bed nets distributed • Documentation of HDA activities • Proportion of outpatient services, antenatal services, fever treatment services, acute respiratory infection (ARI) treatment services, and contraceptive methods delivery that are provided by health posts/HEWs
Intermediary factors	
Material circumstances	• Proportion of households with access to improved sources of drinking water • Proportion of households with improved sanitation facilities • Proportion of women reporting to have disposed of children's stools in safe ways
Socioeconomic and psychological circumstances	• % of women having heard about HIV/AIDS • % of women having knowledge about HIV-prevention methods • % of women with accepting attitudes toward those living with HIV/AIDS • % of women with knowledge about contraceptive methods
Behavioral and biological factors	• % of children with vaccination • % of women currently using modern contraceptive methods • % of pregnant women receiving HIV counseling during antenatal care • Initial breastfeeding within one hour or one day after birth • Feeding practice (consuming iron-rich food) • % of households with iodized salt
Services minimizing consequence of diseases or life events on health	• % of pregnant women receiving antenatal care • % of pregnant women with skilled birth attendance • % of children with fever seeking care from health providers • % of children with ARI seeking care from health providers • % of mothers with knowledge of ORS • % of children given vitamin A supplements

Source: Authors' generation.
Note: HEWs = health extension workers; HDA = health development army; AIDS = acquired immune deficiency syndrome; HIV = human immunodeficiency virus; ORS = oral rehydration solution.

Table 3.2 Sample Information about EDHS 2005 and EDHS 2011

	EDHS 2005	EDHS 2011
Response rate (%)	98.5 for households 96.2 for eligible women	98.1 for households 95.0 for eligible women
Sample size	13,721 households 14,070 women age 15–49	16,702 households 16,515 women age 15–49
Field work	April 27 to August 30, 2005	December 2010 to June 2011

Sources: CSA and ICF International 2006, 2012.

This study uses multiple existing data sources. FMOH annual performance reports, FMOH policy documents, Demographic Health Survey (DHS) data are used for HEP outputs. A 2012 household survey on service utilization and expenditure is used for proportion of outpatient services provided by HEWs. DHS data (2005 and 2011) are used for results on level and distribution of intermediary factors and health outcomes. We believe it is appropriate to use data from DHS 2005 and 2010 for examining the contribution of HEWs to move toward universal health coverage for two reasons: (1) DHS data have been considered the golden standard in developing countries for service coverage and health outcomes; and (2) the period between the two surveys (2005 to 2010) happens to be the first few years after HEP became operational in 2004. Table 3.2 presents basic sample information about these two surveys.

Results

HEP Outputs
Deployment of Health Extension Workers
The HEP has made significant progress in deploying health extension workers and improving availability of health human resources. Figure 3.3 shows that the deployment of HEWs increased steadily over time. By 2009/10, more than 34,000 HEWs were deployed, surpassing the target of 30,000. The deployment of HEWs greatly increased availability of health human resources in the country. As of 2009/10, there was only one physician for every 36,000 population and one midwife for every 56,000 population. With HEWs, the population-to-health workforce ratio has more than halved from 3,038 to 1,394 (figure 3.4). The ratio has decreased more in rural and pastoral regions. In Somali region one health worker could have been serving more than 10,000 people without HEWs; the deployment of HEWs brought down the ratio to about 1 to 3,000. Table B.2 in appendix B also presents detailed data on availability of health human resources by region and type of health workers.

Training and Graduation of Model Families
Training and graduation of model families started in 2006/07 and peaked during the period between 2008/09 and 2010/11. By 2010/11, more than 12 million

Figure 3.3   Cumulative Number of HEWs, by Year

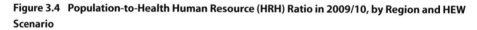

Source: FMOH 2004, 2006, 2007a, 2008a, 2009.
Note: HEW = health extension worker.

Figure 3.4   Population-to-Health Human Resource (HRH) Ratio in 2009/10, by Region and HEW Scenario

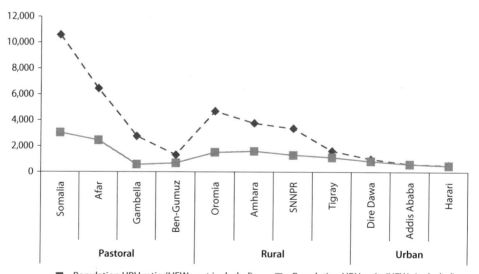

Source: FMOH administrative data (2009/10) and Ethiopia census data (2007).
Note: HEWs = health extension workers.

households graduated as model families (table 3.3), covering 70 percent of eligible households (figure 3.5). The percentage of model families varies greatly by region with a range between 85 percent in Oromia region and 0 percent in Gambella region, and is much higher in rural regions than in urban and pastoral regions.

Table 3.3 Cumulative Number of Model Families Graduated as of 2010/11, by Residence

	Urban	Agrarian	Pastoral	Total
2006/07	240	64,966	1,626	66,832
2007/08	848	818,133	9,476	828,457
2008/09	848	4,041,592	19,092	4,061,532
2009/10	4,559	9,928,923	46,224	9,979,706
2010/11	63,355	11,978,032	137,243	12,178,630

Source: FMOH 2006, 2007a, 2008a, 2009, 2010a.

Figure 3.5 Coverage of Model Families as of 2010/11, by Region

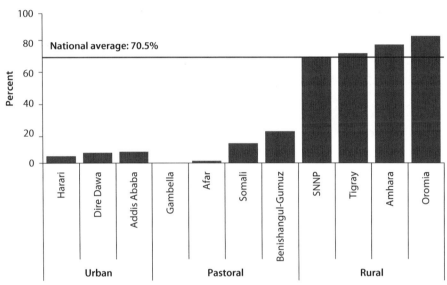

Source: FMOH 2010a.

Organization and Mobilization of Health Development Army

The organization and mobilization of the HDA started in Tigray and Southern Nations, Nationalities and Peoples' (SNNP) regions in 2010/11, and was expanded to other regions to capacitate families who were lagging behind in adopting safe health practices. Table 3.4 shows the progress in mobilizing HDA by region as of 2012/13; more than 2 million one-to-five networks have been formed in seven regions, implying around 12 million households are captured by the HDA. Box 3.1 documents observations of HDA from a rapid supervision visit in Tigray, showing innovative activities conducted by HDA groups to remove bottlenecks in utilizing essential services.

Ethiopia Health Extension Program · http://dx.doi.org/10.1596/978-1-4648-0815-9

Table 3.4 Progress in Organization and Mobilization of HDA as of 2013/14

Regions	Number of HDA groups	Number of one-to-five networks
Tigray	29,849	149,245
SNNP	84,129	626,953
Amhara	118,625	572,802
Oromia	195,846	880,975
Addis Ababa	10,407	41,561
Harari	1,613	5,510
Dire Dawa	2,286	59,766
National	442,755	2,336,812

Source: FMOH 2013a.
Note: HDA = health development army.

Box 3.1 Observations from a Rapid Supervision of HDA in Tigray

A team composed of high-level officials from the Ministry of Health and regional health bureaus visited some woredas of Tigray, Amhara, Oromia, and SNNP regions in late 2011. During the visit, the women-centered HDA in Tigray were disciplined in having regular meetings, identifying salient problems in the local context, and proposing and implementing the strategies to address those problems. They also ranked each woman based on implementation of the HEP. As a consequence of female focus, better participation of married women was observed in Tigray than in the other regions.

This visit has also observed some innovations introduced by women's groups that have started to positively influence women's choice of place for childbirth in Tigray. Below are some examples:

1. Preparation of porridge in health facilities: There is a deep-rooted cultural belief in Tigray that would require a mother to eat porridge after giving birth. If a mother does not have access to porridge, it is believed that evil things could happen to either the mother or her newborn. Hence, women prefer to give birth at home. The HDA has started to prepare porridge in health facilities if a woman from their team is in labor.
2. Traditional ambulance: In Tigray the terrain poses a significant challenge. The HDA came up with a locally made stretcher and also organized the youth to carry a laboring mother to the nearby health facility or major road where the regular ambulance could be accessed.
3. Monthly conferences with all pregnant women in the village: The HDA has played a critical role in commencing a monthly conference with all pregnant women, facilitated by HEWs and midwives from the Primary Health Care Unit. The conferences are used to improve peer-to-peer support.
4. Dialogue with traditional birth attendants (TBAs): Since the majority of TBAs are women, it is easier for them to convince laboring mothers to deliver babies at health facilities instead of at home.

Source: FMOH 2013b.

Service Provision by HEWs

Disseminating family planning messages: Based on available information, community events have become the number one source (36.7 percent) of family planning messages for people at reproductive age; this includes all community activities conducted by HEWs and model families (figure 3.6).

Figure 3.6   Exposure to Family Planning Messages, from 2005 to 2011

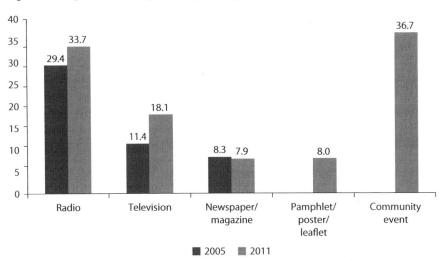

Sources: CSA and ICF International 2006, 2012.
Note: Exposure to family planning messages in this figure is measured as percentage of women and men age 15–49 who heard or saw a family planning message from different sources in the past few months.

General outpatient visits: HEWs on average provided about 35 percent of outpatient visits in the whole country. This percentage is higher particularly among people with less education (about 41 percent) compared with people with grade 10 and above education (about 12 percent), and among the lowest wealth quintile (about 41 percent) compared with highest wealth quintile (about 25 percent).

Provision of selected services: HEWs play a significant role in many services that are critical for child and reproductive health. According to the results from EDHS 2011, HEWs are sources of modern contraceptives for more than 25 percent of users, 17 percent of antenatal service users, 12 percent for diarrhea treatment, and 8 percent for fever treatment among children who sought treatment. More importantly, people who receive these services are rural, less educated, and poor (table 3.5).

Material Circumstances

Improved sanitation: Access to better sanitation facilities has been improved. DHS data show that the percentage of households with improved sanitation facilities has increased from 4.9 to 6.6 percent in rural areas. This may not appear to be a substantial increase, but is a significant achievement compared to the situation in urban areas, where this indicator dropped from 18.0 to 14.1 percent (figure 3.7). Improvement in rural areas is consistent with progress in latrine construction under the HEP. As of 2012/13, the cumulative number of households with latrines was more than 15 million, with coverage being 86 percent.

Table 3.5 Background Characteristics of Users of Selected Services Provided by HEWs

	Fever treatment (%)	Diarrhea treatment (%)	Antenatal care (%)	Contraceptives (%)
Residence				
Rural	98.3	98.5	99.8	99.6
Urban	1.7	1.5	0.2	0.4
Education level				
No education	67.5	71.4	77.1	72.8
Primary	28.8	25.6	1.7	25.3
Secondary or higher	3.7	3.0	0.7	1.8
Wealth quintile				
Lowest	24.4	25.1	28.9	24.2
Secondary	21.3	20.3	27.1	25.4
Middle	21.8	20.1	24.2	25.1
Fourth	18.7	21.8	18.1	21.7
Highest	13.9	12.8	1.7	3.6

Source: EDHS 2011.

Figure 3.7 Access to Improved Sanitation Facilities, from 2005 to 2011

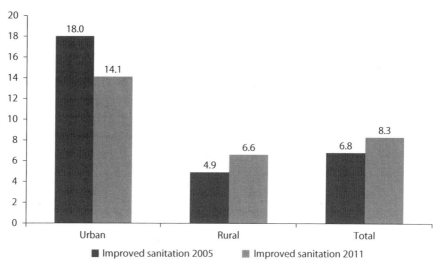

Sources: CSA and ICF International 2006, 2012.
Note: A household is classified as having an improved toilet if it is used only by members of one household (that is, it is not shared), and if the facility used by the household separates the waste from human contact. This figure presents the percentage of households with improved sanitation facilities by residence.

Disposal of children's stools: More mothers have knowledge about proper ways of disposing of children's stools. As of 2011, 36 percent of under-five children's stools were disposed of safely, which is close to a 70 percent increase compared to 2005. In addition, when looking at the relative change from 2005 to 2011, the biggest improvements happened in rural areas (69 percent), among mothers without education (78 percent), and in the lowest quintile (133 percent). A strong gradient is observed for both education and wealth status as shown in figure 3.8 and table B.3. The concentration curves in figure 3.8 also show an improvement in equity for this indicator from 2005 to 2011.

Socioeconomic and Psychological Circumstances

Knowledge about HIV/AIDS: Knowledge about HIV/AIDS has improved in the period from 2005 to 2011. Relative changes from 2005 to 2011 (see figure 3.9 and table B.4) show bigger improvements in rural areas than in urban areas (8.6 vs. 0.6), a strong gradient with education level (9.8 for no education and 0 for

Figure 3.8 Knowledge of Proper Ways of Disposing of Children's Stools, from 2005 to 2011

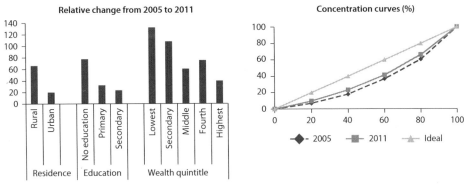

Source: EDHS 2005 and EDHS 2011.
Note: Relative change from 2005 to 2011 (%) shown in left panel are based on table B.3.

Figure 3.9 Knowledge about HIV/AIDS, from 2005 to 2011

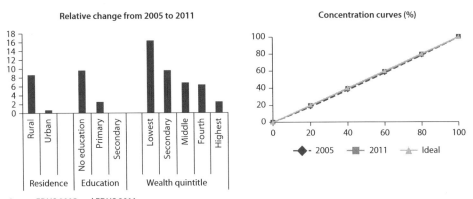

Source: EDHS 2005 and EDHS 2011.
Note: Relative change from 2005 to 2011 (%) shown in left panel are based on table B.4.

secondary education), and a strong gradient for wealth status (16.3 for lowest quintile and 2.5 for highest). Concentration curves do not show any inequality in this regard for both 2005 and 2011.

Knowledge of HIV-prevention methods: Knowledge of HIV-prevention methods has improved from 2005 to 2011. Relative changes from 2005 to 2011 (figure 3.10 and table B.5) show bigger improvement in rural areas than in urban areas (35.0 vs. –7.5), a strong gradient with education level (31.1 for no education and –12.2 for secondary education), and a strong gradient for wealth status (69.8 for lowest quintile and 4.5 for highest). The concentration curves in figure 3.10 also show an improvement in equity for this indicator from 2005 to 2011.

Accepting attitude toward those living with HIV/AIDS: In relation to HEP activities, significantly more women expressed accepting attitudes toward living with people with HIV/AIDS in the period from 2005 to 2011. Relative changes from 2005 to 2011 (figure 3.11 and table B.6) show bigger improvements in

Figure 3.10   Knowledge of HIV-Prevention Methods, from 2005 to 2011

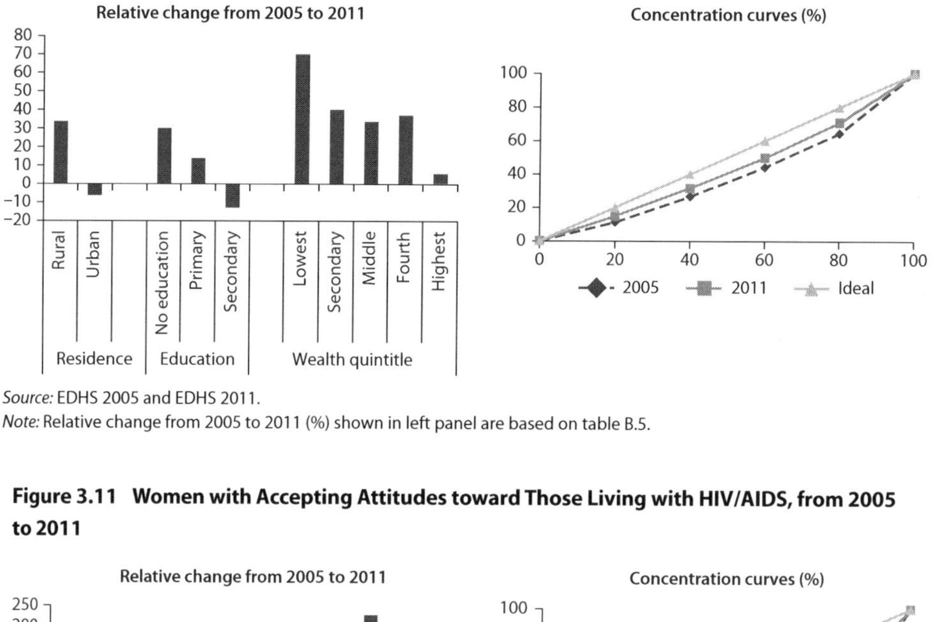

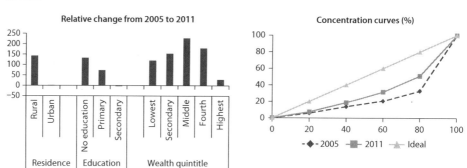

Source: EDHS 2005 and EDHS 2011.
Note: Relative change from 2005 to 2011 (%) shown in left panel are based on table B.5.

Figure 3.11   Women with Accepting Attitudes toward Those Living with HIV/AIDS, from 2005 to 2011

Source: EDHS 2005 and EDHS 2011.
Note: Relative change from 2005 to 2011 (%) shown in left panel are based on table B.6.

rural areas than in urban areas (141.9 vs. 1.3 percent), and a strong gradient with education level (132.4 percent for no education and –4.1 percent for secondary education). For wealth status, the biggest improvement happens in the middle (227 percent) and fourth (180 percent) quintiles, and the least in the highest quintile (28 percent). The concentration curves in figure 3.11 also show an improvement in equity for this indicator from 2005 to 2011.

Knowledge about contraceptive methods: Women's knowledge about contraceptive methods has improved in terms of the percentage of women who have heard of any contraceptive method. Slightly more improvement is seen for currently married women than for sexually active unmarried women (11.5 vs. 9.4 percent). Moreover, their knowledge about specific methods has increased substantially, particularly for female sterilization, male sterilization, implants, and standard day methods. For example, about 70 percent of currently married women had heard of implants in 2011, compared with only 20 percent in 2005 (table 3.6).

Table 3.6 Knowledge about Contraceptive Methods, from 2005 to 2011

	Sexually active unmarried women			Currently married women		
	2005 (%)	2011 (%)	Relative change from 2005 to 2011 (%)	2005 (%)	2011 (%)	Relative change from 2005 to 2011 (%)
Any method	91.2	99.8	9.4	87.5	97.6	11.5
Any modern method	91.2	99.7	9.3	87.4	97.4	11.4
Female sterilization	30.4	50.8	**67.1**	17.2	39.8	**131.4**
Male sterilization	12.5	21.4	**71.2**	5.5	10.8	**96.4**
Pill	86.8	96.4	11.1	84.2	92.6	10.0
IUD	33.0	36.7	11.2	12.2	26.4	**116.4**
Injectables	87.4	98.3	12.5	82.6	96.1	16.3
Implants	47.3	81.9	**73.2**	20.0	69.2	**246.0**
Male condom	69.8	92.3	32.2	40.6	78.1	**92.4**
Female condom	0.0	54.9	n.a.	0.0	27.3	n.a.
Lactational Amenorrhea Method (LAM)	20.9	3.5	−83.3	8.9	2.6	−70.8
Emergency contraception	0.0	41.0	n.a.	0.0	16.0	n.a.
Diaphragm/foam/jelly	4.5	0.0	−100.0	4.4	0.0	−100.0
Standard days method	4.7	14.3	**204.3**	3.4	10.8	**217.6**
Any traditional method	53.2	77.3	45.3	17.0	47.4	**178.8**
Rhythm	48.2	70.3	45.9	14.4	41	**184.7**
Withdrawal	28.6	47.5	**66.1**	9.3	24.5	**163.4**
Other	0.0	1.6	n.a.	0.6	0.9	50.0

Sources: CSA and ICF International 2006, 2012.
Note: This table presents the percentage of currently married respondents, and sexually active unmarried respondents age 15 to 49 who have heard of any contraceptive method, by specific method; n.a. = not applicable.

Behavioral and Biological Factors

Vaccination: There has been some improvement in coverage of vaccination; more improvement is observed in rural areas than in urban areas, but the trends by education level and wealth level are almost opposite, with more educated groups and wealthier groups having bigger improvements. The concentration curves in figure 3.12 show that the equity of this indicator became worse from 2005 to 2011. Detailed results on change of coverage are presented in table B.7.

Use of contraceptive methods: Substantial progress has been made in the use of modern contraceptive methods. Women currently using modern methods doubled from 2005 to 2014. The trend of relative changes shows a stronger improvement in rural areas than in urban areas, and a strong education gradient and a strong income gradient, see table B.8. The concentration curves in figure 3.13 also show an improvement in equity for this indicator from 2005 to 2011 and in 2014.

Figure 3.12 Coverage of Vaccinations, from 2005 to 2011

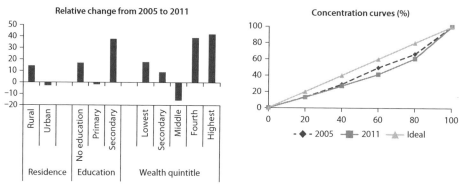

Source: EDHS 2005 and EDHS 2011.
Note: Coverage of vaccination is the proportion of under-two-year-olds fully vaccinated. Relative change from 2005 to 2011 (%) shown in left panel is based on table B.7.

Figure 3.13 Use of Modern Contraceptive Methods, from 2005 to 2014

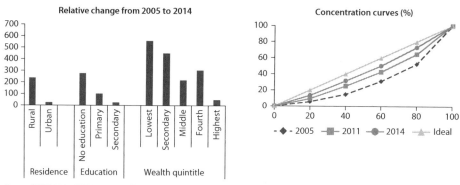

Source: EDHS 2005, EDHS 2011, and EMDHS 2014.
Note: Relative change from 2005 to 2014 (%) shown in left panel are based on table B.8.

Initial breastfeeding: There is a decline in the level of initial breastfeeding. The trend by residence, education, and wealth level shows that better-off people have less decrease or slighter increase, while the decrease among disadvantaged groups is much higher (figure 3.14 and table B.9). Concentration curves do not show any inequality in this regard for either 2005 or 2011.

Intake of nutritious food: Young children consuming iron-rich food increased slightly from 11 to 13 percent. Higher percentage of improvement in consuming iron-rich food is observed for poor people and for less educated people (figure 3.15 and table B.10). The concentration curves in figure 3.15 also show a small improvement in equity for this indicator from 2005 to 2011.

Micronutrient intake among children: There is overall increase in percentage of children given vitamin A supplements, from 46 to 53 percent. By socioeconomic group, larger changes happened in the rural (18 percent) and no education (16 percent) groups. Although not a strong gradient, the trend by income groups does show that lower-income groups produce a larger increase relative to higher-income groups (figure 3.16 and table B.11).

Figure 3.14　Initial Breastfeeding, from 2005 to 2011

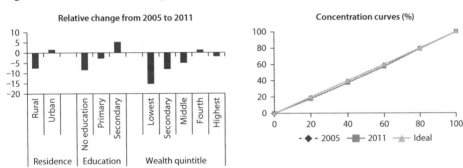

Source: EDHS 2005 and EDHS 2011.
Note: Initial breastfeeding is the proportion of babies breastfed within the first day after birth. Relative change from 2005 to 2011 (%) shown in left panel is based on table B.9.

Figure 3.15　Intake of Nutritious Food by Young Children, from 2005 to 2011

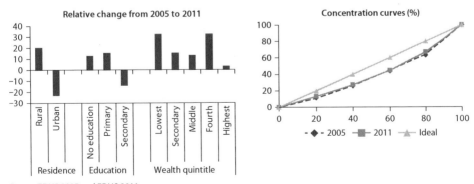

Source: EDHS 2005 and EDHS 2011.
Note: Feeding practice uses the indicator of young children consuming iron-rich food. Relative change from 2005 to 2011 (%) shown in left panel is based on table B.10.

Ethiopia Health Extension Program • http://dx.doi.org/10.1596/978-1-4648-0815-9

Figure 3.16   Micronutrient Intake among Children, from 2005 to 2011

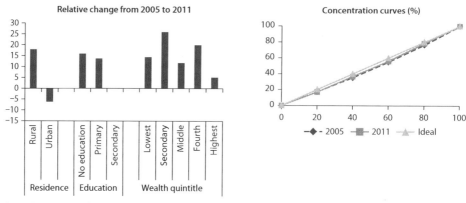

Source: EDHS 2005 and EDHS 2011.
Note: Relative change from 2005 to 2011 (%) shown in left panel is based on table B.11.

Services Minimizing Consequence of Diseases or Life Events on Health

Antenatal care: There has been increase in coverage of antenatal care; however, the change is much smaller if only traditionally defined skilled providers are considered. Figure 3.17 shows that the difference between the richest group and the rest would have been much larger were it not that HEWs provide services that target rural, less educated, and poor women (as shown in table B.12). Not surprisingly, the relative change of antenatal coverage shows strong gradients by residence, education, and wealth level in figure 3.18. The concentration curve also moves toward equity from 2005 to 2011.

HIV counseling during antenatal care: The percentage of women who received HIV counseling more than quadrupled during the period from 2005 to 2011, from 3.1 to 13.6 percent. Although the improvement is impressive across all groups, bigger relative change happened in rural, less educated, and poorer groups (figure 3.19 and table B.14). The concentration curves in figure 3.19 also show an improvement in equity for this indicator from 2005 to 2011.

Skilled birth attendance: Although skilled birth attendance shares similar characteristics with antenatal care, as they are both critical to maternal health, it was not undertaken as much as antenatal care mostly because it requires more sophisticated knowledge and skills. Results in figure 3.20 and table B.15 show that for skilled birth attendance that shares a similar pattern to antenatal care, the concentration curve indicates serious inequality and hardly moved during the period from 2005 to 2011. Data show that higher relative change for disadvantaged groups is due mainly to the critically low level at the starting point.

Treatment of fever: There is an overall increase in the percentage of children with fever seeking care from health professionals. By socioeconomic groups, there were decreases in the urban group and the group with secondary education (about 16 percent), but major changes occurred in the rural (44 percent), no education

Figure 3.17 Coverage of Antenatal Care by Wealth Quintile, from 2005 to 11

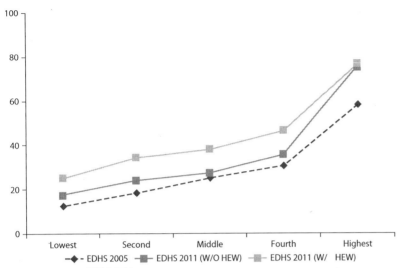

Source: EDHS2005 and EDHS 2011.

Figure 3.18 Coverage of Antenatal Care, from 2005 to 2014

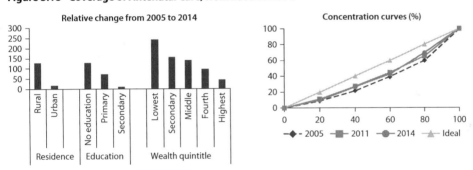

Source: EDHS 2005, EDHS 2011 and EMDHS 2014.
Note: Relative change from 2005 to 2014 (%) shown in left panel is based on table B.12.

Figure 3.19 HIV Counseling during Antenatal Care, from 2005 to 2011

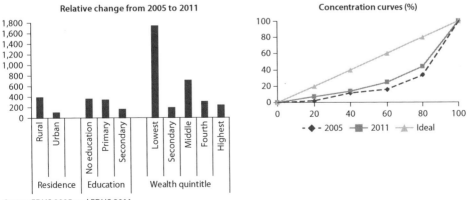

Source: EDHS 2005 and EDHS 2011.
Note: Relative change from 2005 to 2011 (%) shown in left panel is based on table B.14.

Ethiopia Health Extension Program • http://dx.doi.org/10.1596/978-1-4648-0815-9

Figure 3.20   Coverage of Skilled Birth Attendance, from 2005 to 2014

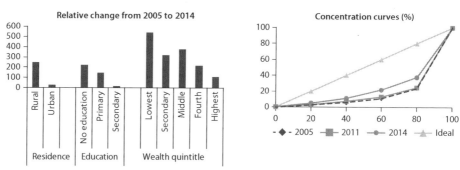

Source: EDHS 2005, EDHS 2011 and EMDHS 2014.
Note: Relative change from 2005 to 2011 (%) shown in left panel is based on table B.15.

(69 percent), and lower-income groups (about 50 percent). The concentration curve of this indicator had a small movement toward equity from 2005 to 2011 (figure 3.21).

Treatment of acute respiratory infection (ARI): Treatment of ARI is similar to treatment for fever, but often tends to get ignored because greater attention is directed toward malaria control. There is an overall increase in percentage of children with ARI symptoms seeking care from health professionals, from 19 to 27 percent. By socioeconomic groups, major changes happened in the rural (45 percent) and no education (60 percent) groups. There is no strong pattern by income groups, but the higher-income group does tend to see more change. The concentration curve in figure 3.22 moves away from the ideal situation during the period between 2005 and 2011 (figure 3.22 and table B.17).

Knowledge of ORS: There is an overall increase in percentage of mothers who have knowledge about ORS, from 46 to 65 percent. By socioeconomic groups, major changes happened in the rural (45 percent) and no education (44 percent) groups. Although there is no strict income gradient, the richest group had the smallest increase compared with other groups(figure 3.23 and table B.18).

Summary of Results

Under the HEP, more than 30,000 HEWs have been deployed, about 70 percent of households have graduated as model families, and more than 300,000 HDA groups were mobilized. HEWs have served a major role in training model families, facilitating HDA mobilization, disseminating health information, and providing basic services. Table 3.7 presents specific results of HEP direct outputs.

While the HEP is being implemented, there has been impressive improvement in material circumstances; socioeconomic, psychological, behavioral, and biological factors; and coverage of services, minimizing consequences of life events and

Figure 3.21 Seeking Treatment for Fever, from 2005 to 2011

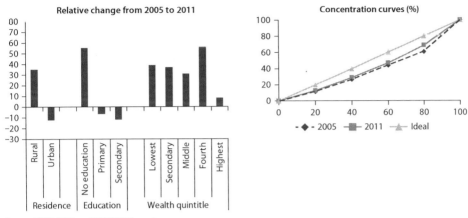

Source: EDHS 2005 and EDHS 2011.
Note: Relative change from 2005 to 2011 (%) shown in left panel is based on table B.16.

Figure 3.22 Seeking Treatment for ARI, from 2005 to 2011

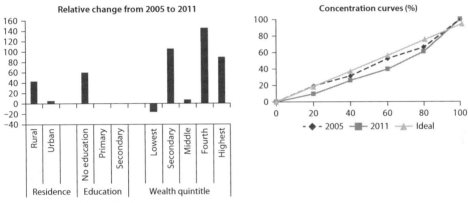

Source: EDHS 2005 and EDHS 2011.
Note: Relative change from 2005 to 2011 (%) shown in left panel is based on table B.17.

Figure 3.23 Knowledge of ORS, from 2005 to 2011

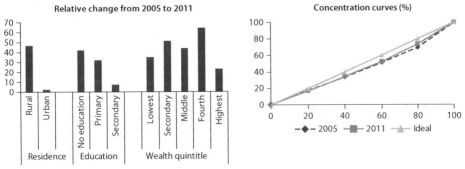

Source: EDHS 2005 and EDHS 2011.
Note: Relative change from 2005 to 2011 (%) shown in left panel is based on table B.18.

diseases. As summarized in table 3.8, most indicators have experienced changes that are pro-rural, pro-less-educated, and pro-poor, and consequently, the concentration index has decreased, and concentration curves have moved toward a more equitable situation. In table 3.8, green cells indicate positive results, meaning the relative change for rural/no education/lowest wealth quintile group is larger than the average, and the concentration curve has moved toward a more equitable scenario. On the other hand, red cells indicate the opposite, meaning the relative change for rural/no education/lowest wealth quintile group is less than the average, and the concentration curve has moved toward a less equitable situation.

Table 3.7 Summary of Results: Health Extension Program Direct Outputs

HEP direct outputs	Results
Number of HEWs deployed	34,382 (2009/10)
Number of model families trained and graduated	12,178,630; 70.5% of all households (2010/11)
Number of HDA mobilized	442,755 HDA groups
Number of latrines constructed	2,289,741 one-to-five networks (2013/14)
Documentation of HDA activities	See box 3.1
	37% through community events
Dissemination of family planning messages	35
Outpatient services provided by HEWs (%)	24
Contraceptives provided by HEWs (%)	17
Antenatal services provided by HEWs (%)	8
Fever treatment services provided by HEWs (%)	12

Source: Data compiled from all the tables and figures in chapter 3.
Note: HEP = Health Extension Program; HEW = health extension worker; HDA = health development army.

Table 3.8 Summary of Results: Intermediary Factors

	DHS results (%)		Relative changes from 2005 to 2011 (%)				Concentration indexes		
	2005	2011	Overall	Rural	No education	Lowest wealth quintile	2005	2011	Pro-equity change
Material circumstance									
Proper disposal of children's stools	21.3	35.8	68.1	69.2	78.0	132.5	0.156	0.120	Yes
Psychological environment									
Women having heard about HIV/AIDS	89.9	96.5	7.3	8.6	9.8	16.3	0.017	0.006	Yes
Women having knowledge about HIV-prevention methods	34.6	43.2	24.9	35.0	31.1	69.8	0.108	0.066	Yes

table continues next page

Table 3.8 Summary of Results: Intermediary Factors (continued)

	DHS results (%)		Relative changes from 2005 to 2011 (%)				Concentration indexes		
	2005	2011	Overall	Rural	No education	Lowest wealth quintile	2005	2011	Pro-equity change
Women with accepting attitudes toward those living with HIV/AIDS	10.7	17.1	59.8	141.9	132.4	120.0	0.255	0.184	Yes
Biological and behavioral factors									
Women currently using modern contraceptive methods	13.9	27.3	96.4	112.3	122.4	225.0	0.192	0.063	Yes
Women currently using modern contraceptive methods (2014 data)[a]	13.9	58.4	190.6	250.9	253.1	577.5			Yes
Children with full vaccination	20.4	24.3	19.1	14.0	16.9	19.1	0.083	0.115	No
Initial breastfeeding within one day after birth	85.7	80.2	-6.4	-7.4	-8.4	-15.2	0.001	0.016	No
Intake of iron-rich food	11.3	13.3	17.7	20.2	16.7	33.3	0.111	0.096	Yes
Children given vitamin A supplements	45.8	53.1	15.9	18.0	15.5	14.4	0.034	0.024	Yes
Services minimizing consequences of life events and diseases									
Pregnant women receiving antenatal care	27.6	42.6	54.3	54.0	56.2	97.6	0.141	0.104	Yes
Pregnant women receiving antenatal care (2014 data)[a]	27.6	58.4	111.6	130.0	129.5	244.1			Yes
Pregnant women receiving HIV counseling during antenatal care	3.1	13.6	338.7	394.1	373.3	1666.7	0.275	0.220	Yes
Skilled birth attendance	5.7	10.0	75.4	53.8	100.0	142.9	0.314	0.304	Yes
Skilled birth attendance (2014 data)[a]	5.7	15.5	171.9	250.0	226.1	542.9	0.314	0.249	Yes
Children with fever seeking care from health providers	17.5	24.2	38.3	43.6	68.5	48.1	0.115	0.087	Yes
Children with ARI seeking care from health providers	18.7	27.0	44.4	44.5	59.7	-16.7	0.061	0.127	No
Mothers with knowledge of oral rehydration solution (ORS)	46.2	65.2	41.1	44.5	43.5	34.1	0.057	0.046	Yes

Source: Data compiled from all the tables and figures from chapter 3.
Note: AIDS = acquired immune deficiency syndrome; HIV = human immunodeficiency virus; ARI = acute respiratory infection. a. 2014 data are available for three indicators (coverage of antenatal care, skilled birth attendance, and contraceptives). Therefore, 2014 data are cited in the column for 2011 for these rows to compare with 2005 data.

Note

1. Wealth status is measured by wealth index quintiles that are constructed based on household asset data via a principal components analysis. It serves as an indicator of level of wealth that is consistent with expenditure and income measures (Rutstein 1999).

CHAPTER 4

Discussions

Contribution of HEP to UHC

It is indeed challenging to estimate precisely the impact of Health Extension Program (HEP) on the progress toward universal health coverage (UHC), as there is no counterfactual information available for comparison purposes when such a national program is at discussion. The contribution of HEP to UHC, however, can be validated through a number of perspectives described below.

First, there are expected changes at each link of the results chain and among the underserved population groups that HEP targets, as shown in chapter 3. For example, at the results chain of reducing wasting, chapter 3 has documented increase of improved sanitation facilities, and increase in women's knowledge of properly dealing with children's stool and of using ORS for children with diarrhea.

Second, health extension workers (HEWs) have served as a major source of health information (for example, family planning message) and service provision including antenatal care, family planning, and general outpatient service (fever and diarrhea treatment).

Third, HEP is the most important intervention undertaken by the government of Ethiopia. There are no alternative interventions that have produced such improvements in material circumstance, knowledge and behavioral factors, and service coverage and outcomes, particularly in rural areas and among poor people.

Lessons for Other Countries

The government of Ethiopia designs and implements the HEP as a living program with different focus at different stages. The HEP builds a work program on the basis of previous achievements so that it can be raised to the next level. As shown in

Figure 4.1, the HEP started with deployment of HEWs after initiation; midway in the deployment in 2007/08, HEWs began training of model families;

Figure 4.1   Focus of the Health Extension Program over Time

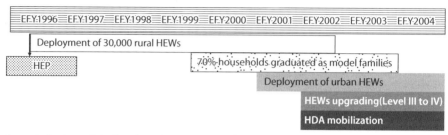

Source: Authors' compilation based on various government documents.
Note: Each colored block is a graphical representation for the period when the majority of the initiative took place.

again, when the training of model families was halfway through, deployment of HEWs to urban areas was started; then when deployment of HEWs and training of model families neared conclusion, upgrading of HEWs and mobilization of health development army (HDA) was begun in 2010/11. Evidently, HDA formation centers around model families and relies on facilitation by HEWs.

The HEP in Ethiopia has demonstrated that an institutionalized community approach is effective for a country to make progress toward UHC. The element of community mobilization identifies community priorities, engages and empowers community members, and solves local problems. The element of institutionalization, on the other hand, addresses the challenge of unsustainability faced by many community programs by ensuring high political commitment, coordinating national policies, and leveraging support from partners. All these may offer valuable lessons for other countries that struggle with similar challenges in the health sector.

Community Mobilization and Empowerment

The HEP is a program deeply rooted in communities. Through this program primary-level preventive services and basic clinical services are provided to communities and households. HEP encourages families to be responsible for their own health by promoting knowledge dissemination and adoption of hygiene practice, feeding practice, appropriate health-seeking behavior from professionals, and proper environmental management. This community outreach ensures sense of ownership and sustainable changes in communities. Communities are actively involved in the implementation of the HEP. As shown in figure 4.1 above, the program penetrated communities stage by stage, from introducing HEWs and training model families, to formation of the heath development army, it thus influenced increasing numbers of people gradually. Communities are part of the selection process of HEWs, which makes HEWs—to the extent possible—stay in communities to carry out their work. They often stay with community households when they conduct home visits, to both save costs and bond with communities. Model families trained under the HEP are given basic knowledge of disease prevention and health promotion. The recently started health development army is an organized mass community mobilization led by Government of Ethiopia (GOE), advocating community participation, piloting innovative activities, and helping to change the socioeconomic and political factors that influence social stratification.

The implementation of HEP benefited from broad community empowerment activities under the Promotion of Basic Services (PBS) supported by multiple development partners including the World Bank. PBS supports a variety of measures designed to improve service quality and local government capacity to manage basic services. These measures range from financial transparency and citizen education in budget issues, to grievance redress mechanisms and social accountability through structured feedback.

- Over the last five years, the Financial Transparency and Accountability (FTA) tools designed under PBS have been rolled out and used to disclose regional- and local-level budget and service delivery information. As a result, more than 90 percent of all woredas and city administrations across the country now post information on local budgets and service delivery targets and accomplishments publicly.
- The Social Accountability program supports civil society organizations that improve opportunities for citizens to provide feedback to local administrators and service providers. The social accountability component piloted Community Score Cards, Citizen Report Cards, and Participatory Budgeting. It also promoted interface meetings between citizens and local authorities to provide feedback on service delivery.
- PBS aims to strengthen existing grievance redress mechanism (GRM) offices[1] at the regional/state level, by contributing to information and public awareness of services they provide, delivering technical assistance to develop a common standard of grievance redress procedure, and capacity development and training for grievance officers. PBS supports the opening of GRM offices in all regions, and of Ethiopian Institution of the Ombudsman (EIO) branch offices, through dialogue and by providing technical and financial support. It is currently financing capacity-building training and workshops conducted by the EIO for regional EIO branch offices and regional GRM officers, and supporting studies to aid the standardization and improvement of the GRM system across the country.
- Recognizing the importance of sound information in improving development outcomes, PBS finances a range of surveys and data collection and management efforts. Capacity-building efforts include financial management and procurement for local woredas, in addition to other needs based on demand.

Political Commitment

The HEP is a long-term commitment by the government of Ethiopia. From its inception in 2003/04, it has lived through three changes of leadership in the Ministry of Health and one in the leadership of the country itself. Although the specific focus changed over time, it has always been on top of leaders' agendas. Related issues are regularly reviewed and discussed between Federal Ministry of Health (FMOH) and development partners through the Joint Consultative Forum (JCF) co-chaired by the minister of health and the chair of Health, Nutrition and Population (HNP) development partner group. They are also reviewed by FMOH and regional health bureaus in bimonthly regional steering committee meetings chaired by the minister of health.

Instead of standing out as a program that is exceptional to the health system, HEP has been seamlessly integrated into the public health system and sector management. HEWs have formed the base of the pyramid of the public health system, receiving guidance and supervision from health centers, district hospitals, as well as health authorities at all tiers from woreda to central level. The Annual Review Meeting of the health sector, as an important process of assessing past years' performance, and planning next year's work, always includes the HEP as an important component. Each year, new targets are determined by region, and actual results are evaluated against the target. Challenges are also identified for all levels of decision makers to follow up. Box 4.1 lists the challenges identified for HEP implementation and the actions taken to address those challenges; it also points out the importance of ensuring adequate institutionalization.

Box 4.1   Challenges and Actions Taken in HEP Implementation

EFY1999 challenge

- Inadequate institutionalization of HEP in the organizational structure of RHBs, zonal health departments, and woreda health offices. This problem appears to be more prominent in the newly emerging regions
- Inadequate supportive supervision at all levels of the health system
- Delay in the construction of health posts (HPs), especially in Oromia region
- Delay in the fulfillment of equipment and supplies for health posts

EFY1999 actions taken

- Institutionalization of HEP has been taken as an agenda of the regular FMOH-RHB steering committee meeting. It has been discussed thoroughly, and agreement has been reached to give it special attention.
- It is appreciated that the construction of HPs need the support of public administrations; hence, regions will strive to work with them
- Resources have been mobilized from partners to fulfill requirements for medical equipment and supplies for the existing health posts

Source: FMOH 2006.
Note: EFY = Ethiopian fiscal year.

Coordinated National Policies

The implementation of the HEP cannot be successful without a series of national policies creating an enabling socioeconomic and political environment. These include devolution policy, civil service policy, vocational education policy, and health policy.

The power devolution to local governments makes it easier for a community approach to be adopted, as they share principles of local empowerment, participatory governance, demand-responsiveness, administrative autonomy, greater downward accountability, and enhanced local capacity. Ethiopia introduced decentralization as the strategic tool for empowering citizens and devolving power to lower levels, so that a conducive environment could be established to enhance basic service delivery. As a result, a four-tier governance structure was created with the center, the regions, the zones, and the woredas. Within this decentralized context, HEWs were mandated civil servants and included as an integral part of the health service delivery system; their salaries are paid from block grants transferred from Ministry of Finance and Economic Development (MOFED) to regions and woredas. Putting 38,000 people on the payroll is a substantial financial commitment, particularly for a country with limited resources. The fact that this program has been financed for 10 years without major delays has been critical in allowing the program to contribute steadily to UHC.

The HEP has benefited from an innovative collaboration with the Ministry of Education: The Ministry of Health has undertaken the training for health extension workers through their network of technical and vocational training institutions. They developed an occupational standard (See appendix C) and curriculum (see appendices D and E for examples) for each level of the health extension services. After the majority of HEWs were deployed, since 2009, the Open University (OU) UK, in partnership with UNICEF and African Medical Research Foundation, has been supporting the development of an innovative program of print-based blended learning resources to teach the theoretical component and to train HEWs in practical skills in local health centers and district hospitals.

The introduction of HEWs greatly increases availability of health human resources for underserved populations in a short period of time. In rural and remote areas where they are introduced, there is severe shortage of physicians as well as lack of incentives for health professionals to work. They have relatively lower entry bars, receive less training, and work in rural communities. For the types and modalities of services that HEWs provide, people would have chosen other health professionals if they could afford it. For the level of the training, it is also difficult for HEWs to work in other health professional categories, such as nurses, midwives, and physicians. It is worth noting that HEWs were not introduced as a short-term solution, rather with a vision for them to be an integral part of the health system. This is the cornerstone of the HEP that is being institutionalized.

Discussions have taken place on setting policies to develop career paths for HEWs. The government is in the process of upgrading health extension workers from level III to level IV. The core objectives of the upgrading program are to improve the extent and quality of HEP services; to fill gaps identified in previous level III HEP trainings; to improve the knowledge, skill, and attitude of HEWs; to make a significant contribution to achieving the health-related Millennium Development Goals (MDGs); and to upgrade careers of HEWs. Table 4.1 presents the number of HEWs enrolled in an upgrading program.

Equipping HEWs with hardware is indispensable for the implementation of the HEP. With MOFED covering salaries of HEWs, the Ministry of Health focused on capital investment so that all critical inputs could be in the same place and at the same time for service delivery. Training and deployment of HEWs were well coordinated with infrastructure and functionality improvement of health posts. The FMOH also uses resources from the MDG Performance Fund (harmonized support from partners) to provide in-kind transfers, ensuring availability of drugs, commodities, supplies, and capacity-building activities. Figure 4.2 shows

Table 4.1   Number of HEWs Enrolled in an Upgrading Program, by Year

	2010/11	*2011/12*	*2012/13*
Oromia	524	795	1,060
Amhara	235	246	500
SNNP	208	208	290
Tigray	40	40	200
Somali	—	—	106
Dire Dawa	55	45	44
Harari	38	33	40
National	1,100	1,367	2,240

Sources: FMOH 2010a, 2011, 2012a.
Note: — = Not available.

Figure 4.2   Number of Health Posts and HEWs

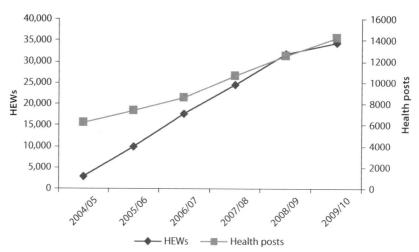

Sources: FMOH 2004, 2005, 2006, 2007a, 2008a, 2009.
Note: HEWs = health extension workers.

that the deployment of HEWs and construction of health posts are progressing in parallel, and that the target of two HEWs per health post was achieved in 2009/10.

Challenges

On the path toward UHC, Ethiopia still faces many challenges. There are challenges in achieving MDG 5 (reducing maternal mortality), expanding some essential interventions such as skilled birth attendance, and improving quality of services provided. The health insurance schemes and management institutions are at their formative stages. A significant number of consultations and capacity-building exercises will be needed along the way to refine scheme designs and enhance implementation capacity. Decision makers and practitioners in the country acknowledge these challenges and are taking active actions to address them. For example, the theme of the 2013 Annual Review Meeting (ARM) was set as "the last lap toward Millennium Development Goals (MDGs): promise renewed to end preventable maternal and child death in Ethiopia." During the meeting, many key issues related to maternal health improvement and service quality enhancement were highlighted.

When this study was undertaken, we identified a few areas that in principle were critical for HEP to contribute toward UHC, but about which almost no information actually exists. This section discusses briefly how these areas may need the attention of policy makers and how best to proceed in these areas.

Quality of Services Provided by HEWs

Quality as an important dimension of UHC is sometimes implicitly assumed or else ignored by policy makers. Without sufficient attention to service quality, both health outcomes and value for money can be compromised. In a context with limited resources, unfortunately, there is a trade-off at times between quantity and quality.

Overall data on quality of services are very limited at the moment. The ongoing 2014 Service Provision Assessment Plus (SPA+) will make information available in this regard once its results are finalized. This is a national facility survey that has two components: a census of all facilities that examine their basic functionalities, and a sample-based facility survey that assesses quality of services, including availability of infrastructure and drugs, efforts of providers, and knowledge of providers based on vignettes.

In spite of limited data, the HEP midterm evaluation 2010 does show that HEWs do not have sufficient knowledge of services they are supposed to provide. For example, HEWs were asked to list the immediate care they give to a newborn while attending a delivery. The responses of HEWs in order of frequency were to initiate breastfeeding within one hour (54 percent); to wipe the face after birth of the head (52.9 percent); to ensure baby is breathing (51.8 percent); to provide cord care with sterile cut 4–6 centimeters from umbilicus (50.4 percent); to provide thermal protection (47.2 percent); to weigh the baby (37.4 percent);

to assess/ examine newborn within one hour (12.3 percent); and to administer eye prophylaxis (11.2 percent).

Results from DHS 2011 and Mini DHS 2014 also indicated the gap in providing quality services. The survey collected information on specific services received during antenatal care by types of providers seen by women. Services included being informed of pregnancy complications, blood sample taken, urine sample taken, taking iron tablets, and taking intestinal parasite drugs. Overall there has been improvement over time in terms of taking blood and urine samples, as well as giving out iron tablets, though the percentage informed of pregnancy complications remains low (figure 4.3). Detailed analysis shows that doctors perform best among all tasks, followed by nurses/midwives, then HEWs. The odds of receiving a package of antenatal services (blood pressure taken, blood sample taken, urine sample taken, complications informed, and iron tablets given) from HEWs is 0.44 smaller than from doctors.

We also examined the treatment used for children with diarrhea by type of providers, as shown in figure 4.4; health facilities (mostly doctors and nurses) fare better for most of these measures except increased fluids and home remedy, which shows that HEWs have potential to do as well as or better than other providers.

While continuing to move toward UHC, it is very important for the government to develop special actions measuring and enhancing quality of services provided by HEWs in the context of overall service quality improvement, so that all people benefiting from HEP—who are mostly disadvantaged groups—will receive equally good quality care as the rest of the society. This can start with systematically understanding the implementation and effectiveness of existing quality enhancement measures such as routine supervisions or refresher courses.

Figure 4.3   Components of Antenatal Care among Receivers, by Type of Providers, from 2005 to 14

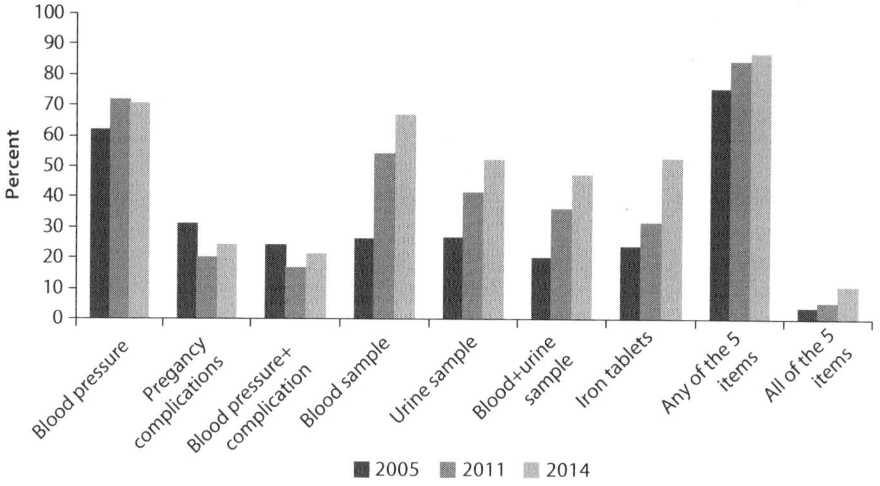

Source: EDHS 2005, EDHS 2011, and Mini DHS 2014.

Figure 4.4   Treatment Used for Children with Diarrhea by Providers in 2011

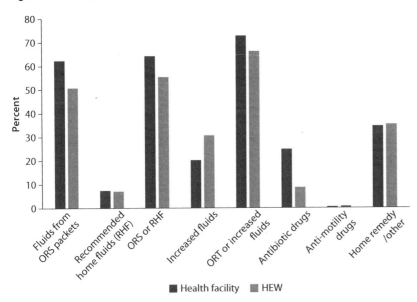

Source: EDHS 2005 and EDHS 2011.
Note: ORS = oral rehydration solution; ORT = oral rehydration therapy; HEW = health extension worker.

The SPA+ has made a good start in assessing facility functionality and providers' knowledge. It will be critical that similar measures are obtained on a regular basis so that effect of actions can be monitored.

Efficiency Improvement

The Health Extension Program by its nature should be an efficient intervention as it is rooted in communities and uses low-cost cadre to provide services. However, there can still be room for improved efficiency as there is wide variation in HEWs' experiences, and more than half of HEWs feel that between 21 and 50 percent of their professional inputs were not utilized because of various constraints.

Based on a survey conducted among a sample of 389 HEWs, the HEP mid-term shows that there is great variation in terms of how HEWs allocate their time, what tasks they focus on, and how long it takes to complete a task. The time allocation pattern to specific HEP services was unbalanced, and mainly focused on a few HEP services. Generally, HEWs spend most of their time on construction, use and maintenance of sanitary latrines, family planning, vaccination services, solid and liquid waste management, and malaria prevention and control. On the other hand, HEWs generally spend less time on adolescent reproductive health; first aid; registration of vital statistics; control of insects, rodents, and other biting species; and tuberculosis prevention and control.

This variation is certainly a combination of community requirements, workload, and HEWs' competencies. The reasons given for not providing certain services include low demand by communities; not a major problem in the village; and lack of skills, time, necessary supplies, and administrative or supervisory support. The majority of HEWs felt that the workload was too much, and required more skill. About 75 percent of HEWs believed they were overloaded with assigned tasks. Moreover, 78.6 percent of HEWs claimed that the type of duties and responsibilities assigned to them require more training than the training they had received.

Systematic and large-scale skills development will be needed for HEWs. There is no doubt that they need to develop skills on providing specific services such as labor monitoring and child growth monitoring. More importantly, given the range of their work and their role in community activities, HEWs need skills development to manage multiple tasks more effectively, to allocate their time more efficiently, to document their work more accurately, and to work with communities more successfully.

Providing a systematic supporting system for HEWs and HDA leaders will also be very important. The major technical challenges in the implementation of HEP according to HEWs were lack of transportation, irregular supply of vaccines and absence of storage and carriage for vaccines, irregular/ no supply of drugs, and lack of adequate skills.

• Upgrading of transportation can save HEWs time on commuting so they spend more time on real work. About 70 percent of within-village transportation is by foot. About 94 percent of transportation between village and district is also by foot. Survey results show that HEWs feel that the best means of transportation within the village and to the district health office would be motorcycle and bicycle. Although the government has taken actions procuring bikes for HEWs, the effect of this practice remains to be studied.

• Upgrading of means of communication and some ready-to-use tools also help carry out work more efficiently. Experiences with mobile health applications show that a smart phone with proper applications would greatly help HEWs communicate with district offices and community members, and keep better records of members' information such as past and upcoming antenatal visits.

• Supportive supervisions need to be enhanced in both frequency and substance so that HEWs can receive timely support and feedback on their work.

Performance Evaluation and Evidence Base Related to HEP

It is understandably difficult to compare overall performance of HEWs between communities, particularly in a quantitative way, because their workload, mix of work program, and community characteristics may be quite different. This raises questions on how to measure workers' performance so that the government can get more value out of this program. Despite the difference in community characteristics and mix of work program, some thought should be given to developing a common set of indicators to monitor workers' performance under HEP so their work can be better aligned with national goals and priorities.

Currently, there is no formal performance evaluation of HEWs on a regular basis; with a fixed salary payment, a rational HEW may opt out in favor of simpler tasks or less responsibility. It is expected that the ongoing Balanced Score Card approach will cover this area at some point. In the Ethiopian context, society relies on peoples' intrinsic motivation to work in rural areas and serve communities. Although paying HEWs' salaries is a great leap forward compared with many other countries with greater resources, a proper performance evaluation and reward to performers can create extrinsic motivation. Performance here translates very generically, and can include quantity of services provided, quality of services provided, and efficiency in providing services.

Note

1. A study conducted in Ethiopia under the auspices of PBS in 2011 found that GRMs exist in several of the country's regions, using different regional-level mechanisms established during the past decade under the government's various programs. However, the mechanisms were set up differently and display significant variations in terms of legal underpinnings, government entity responsible, accountability, procedures, and the finality and enforcement of grievance findings.

Ethiopia Country Fact Data Overview, 2011

Population	*84.7 million*
Gross domestic product (GDP)	US$31.71 billion
Gross national income per capita, Atlas method (current US$)	US$370
Total health expenditure (THE) as percent of GDP	4.65 percent
THE per capita (in current exchange rate dollars)	US$16.6
Out-of-pocket spending as percent of THE	33.8 percent
Public expenditure on health as percent of THE	57.7 percent
Life expectancy at birth	59.2 years
Hospital beds per 1,000 population	6.3

Source: World Development Indicators.

APPENDIX B

Detailed Results

Table B.1 Number and Distribution of Health Centers in EFY2005 (2012/13)

	Number of health centers	Population per health center
Addis Ababa	62	48,000
Dire Dawa	16	24,000
Harari	8	26,000
Afar	62	25,000
Benishangul Gumuz	32	29,000
Gambella	28	13,000
Somali	140	36,000
Amhara	805	23,000
Oromia	1,215	25,000
SNNP	663	25,000
Tigray	214	22,000

Source: FMOH 2012a.
Note: EFY = Ethiopian fiscal year.

Table B.2 Population to Health Work Force Ratio, by Category and Region

Region	Physicians	Health officers	Nurses	Midwives	HEWs
Urban					
Addis Ababa	3,056	16,791	845	11,699	—
Dire Dawa	6,796	18,957	1,324	18,009	4,867
Harari	6,655	6,226	699	6,655	6,031
Rural					
Amhara	58,567	41,024	4,698	83,983	2,775
Oromia	76,075	64,189	5,706	100,197	2,234
SNNP	65,817	72,398	4,002	50,404	2,126
Tigray	44,880	24,111	1,944	24,502	3,600

table continues next page

Table B.2 Population to Health Work Force Ratio, by Category and Region *(continued)*

Region	Physicians	Health officers	Nurses	Midwives	HEWs
Pastoral					
Afar	98,258	50,823	7,967	—	3,930
Benishangul-Gumuz	59,309	16,945	1,575	19,235	1,426
Gambella	25,585	25,585	3,655	83,150	728
Somali	65,817	389,415	14,882	103,844	4,248
National	**36,158**	**48,451**	**3,870**	**56,427**	**2,545**

Source: FMOH administrative data (2009/2010) and Ethiopia census data (2007).
Note: HEWs = health extension workers; — = Not available.

Table B.3 Disposal of Children's Stool (2005–11)

Among Youngest Children under Age Five Living with Their Mothers, Percentage of Children Whose Stools Were Disposed of Safely, by Background Characteristics

Background characteristic	2005 (%)	2011 (%)	Relative change from 2005 to 2011 (%)
Residence			
Urban	51.8	62.5	20.7
Rural	18.5	31.3	69.2
Mother's education			
No education	16.8	29.9	78.0
Primary	33.4	44.6	33.5
Secondary	50.8	63.5	25.0
More than secondary	50.8	75.5	48.6
Wealth quintile			
Lowest	7.7	17.9	132.5
Second	12.3	25.2	104.9
Middle	21.3	34.3	61.0
Fourth	26.6	46.1	73.3
Highest	44.4	63.3	42.6
Total	**21.3**	**35.8**	**68.1**

Source: EDHS 2005 and EDHS 2011.
Note: Children's stools are considered to be disposed of safely if the child used a toilet or latrine, if the fecal matter was put or rinsed into a toilet or latrine, or if it was buried.

Table B.4 Knowledge of HIV/AIDS (2005–11)

Percentage of Women and Men Age 15–49 Who Have Heard of AIDS, by Background Characteristics

Background characteristic	2005 (%)	2011 (%)	Relative change from 2005 to 2011 (%)
Residence			
Urban	98.6	99.2	0.6
Rural	88.0	95.6	8.6

table continues next page

Table B.4 Knowledge of HIV/AIDS (2005–11) *(continued)*

Background characteristic	2005 (%)	2011 (%)	Relative change from 2005 to 2011 (%)
Education			
No education	86.1	94.5	9.8
Primary	95.6	98.1	2.6
Secondary	99.8	99.8	0.0
More than secondary	99.8	100.0	0.2
Wealth quintile			
Lowest	80.4	93.5	16.3
Second	87.8	95.9	9.2
Middle	89.2	95.0	6.5
Fourth	91.5	97.4	6.4
Highest	97.0	99.4	2.5
Total, age 15–49	89.9	96.5	7.3

Source: EDHS 2005 and EDHS 2011.

Table B.5 Knowledge of HIV-Prevention Methods (2005–11)

Women Age 15–49 Who, in Response to Prompted Questions, Say That People Can Reduce the Risk of Getting the AIDS Virus by Using Condoms Every Time They Have Sexual Intercourse, and by Having One Sex Partner Who Is Not Infected and Has No Other Partners, by Background Characteristics

Background characteristic	2005 (%)	2011 (%)	Relative change from 2005 to 2011 (%)
Residence			
Urban	65.5	60.6	−7.5
Rural	28.0	37.8	35.0
Education			
No education	23.5	30.8	31.1
Primary	46.5	52.4	12.7
Secondary	74.3	65.2	−12.2
More than secondary	74.3	73.4	−1.2
Wealth quintile			
Lowest	18.2	30.9	69.8
Second	25.1	35.0	39.4
Middle	28.8	38.1	32.3
Fourth	32.9	44.0	33.7
Highest	58.3	60.9	4.5
Total	**34.6**	**43.2**	**24.9**

Source: EDHS 2005 and EDHS 2011.

Table B.6 Accepting Attitudes toward HIV/AIDS (2005–11)

Among Women Age 15–49 Who Have Heard of AIDS, Percentage Expressing Accepting Attitudes toward People with HIV/AIDS, by Background Characteristics

Background characteristic	2005 (%)	2011 (%)	Relative change from 2005 to 2011 (%)
Residence			
Urban	37.3	37.8	1.3
Rural	4.3	10.4	141.9
Education			
No education	3.4	7.9	132.4
Primary	11.7	20.2	72.6
Secondary	44.1	42.3	−4.1
More than secondary	44.1	52.7	19.5
Wealth quintile			
Lowest	2.5	5.5	120.0
Second	3.4	8.6	152.9
Middle	3.0	9.8	226.7
Fourth	5.3	14.8	179.2
Highest	29.2	37.4	28.1
Total	10.7	17.1	59.8

Source: EDHS 2005 and EDHS 2011.
Note: Accepting attitudes are defined as (1) willing to care for a family member with AIDS; (2) willing to buy fresh vegetables from shopkeeper who has the AIDS virus; (3) saying that a female teacher who has the HIV virus but is not sick should be allowed to continue teaching; and (4) would not want to keep secret that a family member got infected with HIV.

Table B.7 Vaccination (2005–11)

Percentage of Children Age 12–23 Months Who Received DPT3, and All Basic Vaccinations at Any Time before the Survey (According to a Vaccination Card or the Mother's Report), by Background Characteristics

Background characteristic	DPT3			Full vaccination		
	2005 (%)	2011 (%)	Relative change from 2005 to 2011 (%)	2005 (%)	2011 (%)	Relative change from 2005 to 2011 (%)
Residence						
Urban	65.7	60.5	−7.9	49.3	48.1	−2.4
Rural	29.0	32.5	12.1	17.9	20.4	14.0
Mother's education						
No education	27.9	31.2	11.8	17.2	20.1	16.9
Primary	40.7	42.6	4.7	28.6	28.3	−1.0
Secondary	62.2	79.2	27.3	41.5	57.0	37.3
Higher than secondary	62.2	63.9	2.7	41.5	57.7	39.0

table continues next page

Table B.7 Vaccination (2005–11) *(continued)*

Background characteristic	DPT3			Full vaccination		
	2005 (%)	2011 (%)	Relative change from 2005 to 2011 (%)	2005 (%)	2011 (%)	Relative change from 2005 to 2011 (%)
Wealth quintile						
Lowest	25.6	26.0	1.6	14.1	16.8	19.1
Second	26.8	29.4	9.7	16.7	18.2	9.0
Middle	33.0	31.0	−6.1	21.8	18.2	−16.5
Fourth	30.6	42.2	37.9	17.9	24.9	39.1
Highest	47.9	61.5	28.4	35.6	50.5	41.9
Total	31.9	36.5	14.4	20.4	24.3	19.1

Source: EDHS 2005 and EDHS 2011.
Note: All basic vaccinations include BCG, measles, and three doses each of DPT and polio vaccine, excluding polio vaccine given at birth.

Table B.8 Current Use of Modern Contraceptive Methods (2005, 2011, and 2014)

Percentage of Currently Married Women Age 15–49 Using Modern Contraceptives, by Background Characteristics

Background characteristic	2005 (%)	2011 (%)	2014 (%)	Relative change From 2005 to 2011 (%)	Relative change from 2005 to 2014 (%)
Residence					
Urban	42.2	49.5	82.5	17.3	31.8
Rural	10.6	22.5	54.5	112.3	250.9
Education					
No education	9.8	21.8	49.8	122.4	253.1
Primary	21.9	33.7	68.7	53.9	110.0
Secondary	45.9	53.4	90.1	16.3	28.3
Higher than secondary	45.9	57.2	97.0	24.6	41.0
Wealth quintile					
Lowest	4.0	13.0	27.1	225.0	577.5
Second	6.5	21.5	36.3	230.8	458.5
Middle	11.6	24.0	37.3	106.9	221.6
Fourth	15.2	30.3	46.3	99.3	204.6
Highest	33.7	48.2	53.6	43.0	59.1
Total	13.9	27.3	40.4	96.4	190.6

Source: EDHS 2005, EDHS 2011, and EMDHS 2014.
Note: Modern contraceptive methods include female sterilization, male sterilization, pill, IUD, injectable, implants, male condom, female condom, LAM, emergency method, standard days method, and diaphragm/foam/jelly.

Table B.9   Initial Breastfeeding (2005–11)

Among Last-Born Children Who Were Born in the Two Years Preceding the Survey, the Percentages of Those Who Started Breastfeeding within One Day of Birth, by Background Characteristics

Background characteristic	2005 (%)	2011 (%)	Relative change from 2005 to 2011 (%)
Residence			
Urban	81.9	83.2	1.6
Rural	86.1	79.7	−7.4
Mother's education			
No education	86.2	79.0	−8.4
Secondary	81.5	85.8	−5.3
More than secondary	81.5	83.7	2.7
Wealth quintile			
Lowest	85.4	72.4	−15.2
Second	85.5	78.7	−8.0
Middle	85.6	81.3	−5.0
Fourth	86.4	87.6	1.4
Highest	85.8	84.2	−1.9
Total	85.7	80.2	−6.4

Source: EDHS 2005 and EDHS 2011.

Table B.10   Intake of Nutritious Food (2005–11)

Among Youngest Children Age 6–23 Months Who Are Living with Their Mother, the Percentages Who Consumed Iron-Rich Foods in the Day or Night Preceding the Survey, by Background Characteristics

Background characteristic	2005 (%)	2011 (%)	Relative change from 2005 to 2011 (%)
Residence			
Urban	28.7	22.7	−22.3
Rural	9.9	11.9	−20.2
Mother's education			
No education	9.0	10.5	16.7
Primary	14.9	17.4	16.8
Secondary and higher	35.4	30.7	−13.3
	35.4	30.4	−14.1
Wealth quintile			
Lowest	6.9	9.2	33.3
Second	8.7	9.9	13.8
Middle	10.6	12.0	13.2
Fourth	11.6	15.5	33.6
Highest	22.1	23.1	4.5
Total	11.3	13.3	17.7

Source: EDHS 2005 and EDHS 2011.

Table B.11   Vitamin A Supplementation

Among All Children Age 6–59 Months, the Percentages Who Were Given Vitamin A Supplements in the Six Months Preceding the Survey, by Background Characteristics

Background characteristic	2005 (%)	2011 (%)	Relative change from 2005 to 2011 (%)
Residence			
Urban	62.0	56.8	−8.4
Rural	44.5	52.5	18.0
Mother's education			
No education	43.8	50.6	15.5
Primary	50.3	57.4	14.1
Secondary	63.6	63.7	0.2
Higher than secondary	63.6	71.9	13.1
Wealth quintile			
Lowest	39.5	45.2	14.4
Second	42.1	53.2	26.4
Middle	45.6	51.4	12.7
Fourth	49.6	59.6	20.2
Highest	55.4	58.1	4.9
Total	45.8	53.1	15.9

Source: EDHS 2005 and EDHS 2011.

Table B.12   Antenatal Care (2005–11)

Among Women Age 15–49 Who Had a Live Birth in the Five Years Preceding the Survey, Percentage of Those Receiving Antenatal Care from a Skilled Provider for the Most Recent Birth, by Background Characteristics

Background characteristic	2005 (%)	2011 (%) Skilled providers	2011 (%) Skilled providers +HEWs	Relative change from 2005 to 2011 (%) Skilled providers	Relative change from 2005 to 2011 (%) Skilled providers +HEWs
Residence					
Urban	68.9	76.0	76.8	10.3	11.5
Rural	23.7	26.4	36.5	11.4	54.0
Education					
No education	21.7	25.1	33.9	15.7	56.2
Primary	39.4	45.5	55.0	15.5	39.6
Secondary	80.9	85.5	88.5	5.7	9.4
More than secondary	80.9	90.9	93.9	12.4	16.1

table continues next page

Ethiopia Health Extension Program • http://dx.doi.org/10.1596/978-1-4648-0815-9

Table B.12 Antenatal Care (2005–11) *(continued)*

Background characteristic	2005 (%)	2011 (%)		Relative change from 2005 to 2011 (%)	
		Skilled providers	Skilled providers +HEWs	Skilled providers	Skilled providers +HEWs
Wealth quintile					
Lowest	12.7	17.0	25.1	33.9	97.6
Second	18.6	23.7	34.4	27.4	84.9
Middle	25.2	27.0	37.9	7.1	50.4
Fourth	30.6	35.4	46.3	15.7	51.3
Highest	58.0	74.9	76.7	29.1	32.2
Total	27.6	33.9	42.6	22.8	54.3

Source: EDHS 2005 and EDHS 2011.

Note: Skilled antenatal provider includes doctor, nurse, or midwife. HEWs = health extension workers.

Table B.13 Antenatal Care (2005–14)

Among Women Age 15–49 Who Had a Live Birth in the Five Years Preceding the Survey, Percentage of Those Receiving Antenatal Care from a Skilled Provider for the Most Recent Birth, by Background Characteristics

Background characteristic	2005 (%)	2014 (%)		Relative change from 2005 to 2014 (%)	
		Skilled providers	Skilled providers +HEWs	Skilled providers	Skilled providers +HEWs
Residence					
Urban	68.9	80.3	82.5	16.5	19.7
Rural	23.7	40.8	54.5	72.2	130.0
Education					
No education	21.7	32.0	49.8	47.5	129.5
Primary	39.4	50.5	68.7	28.2	74.4
Secondary	80.9	81.9	90.1	1.2	11.4
More than secondary	80.9	96.3	97.0	19.0	19.9
Wealth quintile					
Lowest	12.7	23.7	43.7	86.6	244.1
Second	18.6	29.3	48.0	57.5	158.1
Middle	25.2	40.6	60.8	61.1	141.3
Fourth	30.6	42.2	60.9	37.9	99.0
Highest	58.0	77.3	84.2	33.3	45.2
Total	27.6	41.2	58.4	49.3	111.6

Source: EDHS 2005 and EMDHS 2014.

Note: Skilled antenatal provider includes doctor, nurse, or midwife. HFWs = health extension workers.

Table B.14 HIV Counseling during Antenatal Care (2005–11)

Among All Women Age 15–49 Who Gave Birth in the Two Years Preceding the Survey, the Percentage Who Received HIV Counseling during Antenatal Care, by Background Characteristics

Background characteristic	2005 (%)	2011 (%)	Relative change from 2005 to 2011 (%)
Residence			
Urban	20.0	46.8	134.0
Rural	1.7	8.4	394.1
Education			
No education	1.5	7.1	373.3
Primary	4.5	20.4	353.3
Secondary	24.1	62.8	160.6
Higher than secondary	24.1	71.7	197.5
Wealth quintile			
Lowest	0.3	5.3	1,666.7
Second	1.8	5.5	205.6
Middle	0.8	8.1	912.5
Fourth	3.4	14.6	329.4
Highest	12.3	42.8	248.0
Total	3.1	13.6	338.7

Source: EDHS 2005 and EDHS 2011.

Table B.15 Skilled Birth Attendance (2005, 2011, and 2014)

Among Women Who Had Births in the Five Years Preceding the Survey, Percentage of Births Assisted by a Skilled Provider, by Background Characteristics

Background characteristic	2005 (%)	2011 (%)	2014 (%)	Relative change from 2005 to 2011 (%)	Relative change from 2005 to 2014 (%)
Residence					
Urban	44.6	50.8	58.4	13.9	30.9
Rural	2.6	4.0	9.1	53.8	250.0
Mother's education					
No education	2.3	4.6	7.5	100.0	226.1
Primary	8.5	15.4	21.0	81.2	147.1
Secondary	57.7	72.4	69.4	25.5	20.3
Higher than secondary	57.7	74.1	90.7	28.4	57.2
Wealth quintile					
Lowest	0.7	1.7	4.5	142.9	542.9
Second	1.3	2.9	5.5	123.1	323.1

table continues next page

Table B.15 Skilled Birth Attendance (2005, 2011, and 2014) *(continued)*

Background characteristic	2005 (%)	2011 (%)	2014 (%)	Relative change from 2005 to 2011 (%)	Relative change from 2005 to 2014 (%)
Middle	1.9	3.2	9.1	68.4	378.9
Fourth	4.5	7.4	14.5	64.4	222.2
Highest	26.6	45.6	55.6	71.4	109.0
Total	5.7	10.0	15.5	75.4	171.9

Source: EDHS 2005, EDHS 2011, and EMDHS 2014.

Table B.16 Seeking Care for Fever (2005–11)

Among Children under Age Five Who Had a Fever in the Two Weeks Preceding the Survey, Percentage for Whom Advice or Treatment Was Sought from a Health Facility or Provider, by Background Characteristics

Background characteristic	2005 (%)	2011 (%)	Relative change from 2005 to 2011 (%)
Residence			
Urban	45.3	37.8	−16.6
Rural	15.6	22.4	43.6
Mother's education			
No education	13.0	21.9	68.5
Primary	29.4	27.1	−7.8
Secondary	53.9	45.1	−16.3
More than secondary	53.9	(43.6)	−180.9
Wealth quintile			
Lowest	10.8	16.0	48.1
Second	14.2	20.9	47.2
Middle	16.6	23.1	39.2
Fourth	16.4	28.1	71.3
Highest	37.0	40.4	9.2
Total	17.5	24.2	38.3

Source: EDHS 2005 and EDHS 2011.
Note: Pharmacy, drug vendor/store, shop, and traditional healer are not considered health facility or provider.

Table B.17 Seeking Care for ARI (2005–11)

Among Children under Age Five Who Had Symptoms of Acute Respiratory Infection (ARI) in the Two Weeks Preceding the Survey, Percentage for Whom Advice or Treatment Was Sought from a Health Facility or Provider, by Background Characteristics

Background characteristic	2005 (%)	2011 (%)	Relative change from 2005 to 2011 (%)
Residence			
Urban	45.6	46.9	2.9
Rural	17.3	25.0	44.5

table continues next page

Table B.17 Seeking Care for ARI (2005–11) *(continued)*

Background characteristic	2005 (%)	2011 (%)	Relative change from 2005 to 2011 (%)
Mother's education			
No education	15.4	24.6	59.7
Primary	27.6	27.7	0.4
Secondary	(50.1)	..	
		..	
Wealth quintile			
Lowest	18.6	15.5	−16.7
Second	12.3	25.2	104.9
Middle	20.7	22.1	6.8
Fourth	13.2	33.2	151.5
Highest	33.1	61.7	86.4
Total	18.7	27.0	44.4

Source: EDHS 2005 and EDHS 2011.
Note: .. = Negligible: sample size too small to estimate.

Table B.18 Knowledge of Oral Rehydration Solution (ORS) Packets (2005–11)

Percentage of Mothers Who Gave Birth in the Five Years Preceding the Survey Who Know about ORS Packets or Prepackaged Liquids for Treatment of Diarrhea, by Background Characteristics

Background characteristic	2005 (%)	2011 (%)	Relative change from 2005 to 2011 (%)
Residence			
Urban	85.3	86.5	1.4
Rural	42.5	61.4	44.5
Mother's education			
No education	41.4	59.4	43.5
Primary	55.7	73.8	32.5
Secondary	88.9	93.7	5.4
Higher than secondary	88.9	98.2	10.5
Wealth quintile			
Lowest	41.1	55.1	34.1
Second	39.2	59.0	50.5
Middle	41.0	59.4	44.9
Fourth	42.4	69.4	63.7
Highest	73.1	88.4	20.9
Total	46.2	65.2	41.1

Source: EDHS 2005 and EDHS 2011.

Example of Occupational Standard for Health Extension Service Level III: Antenatal Care

Occupational Standard: Health Extension Service Level III	
Unit Title	Promote and Provide Antenatal Care
Unit Code	HLT HES3 07 0213
Unit Descriptor	This unit describes the competency required to provide antenatal examination and advice, and conduct early referral of cases with abnormalities and/or complications during pregnancy and delivery.

Element	Performance Criteria
1. Provide antenatal examination and information for pregnant women	1.1 General, social, and obstetric health history are taken and documented to deliver health care.
	1.2 Symptoms of pregnancy are identified. Antenatal care plan is prepared in consultation with the pregnant woman based on standard protocols and client requirements.
	1.3 Information on healthy living and maternal health are discussed.
	1.4 **Antenatal examination** is performed in line with standard protocols and client requirements.
	1.5 **Information** on birthing options, signs and stages of labor, pain management techniques, and family attendance at delivery are provided for client.
	1.6 Sign and symptoms of minor disorders of pregnancy and **potential serious complications** are identified to provide advice and refer to the next level.
	1.7 Information is provided on prevention of mother-to-child transmission (PMTCT) of HIV.
	1.8 Women are supported to obtain the necessary medicines and are provided with appropriate information on use.
2. Conduct home visit and refer pregnant women with health problems	2.1 Registers of women undergoing antenatal care are maintained according to organization policies and procedure.
	2.2 Schedules of participation in antenatal care and use are kept to organize continuing care for women.
	2.3 Reminders and other assistance are organized and/or provided for women to attend antenatal care according to their needs.
	2.4 Referral and communication networks with medical staff, midwives, allied health staff, birthing facilities, and female community elders are maintained.
	2.5 Records on attendance for antenatal care and birthing outcomes are kept and used to follow antenatal care.

Variables	Range
1. Risk factors include:	• Lifestyle and other health problems identified from a health history • Potential effects of health-related problems on the fetus, including: • Alcohol consumption • Tobacco use • Malnutrition • Prescription and nonprescription drugs • Drugs that are not prescribed • Environmental hazards • Potential impact of compliance or noncompliance with antenatal care plan • Presence or absence of family, financial, and social support systems • Environmental and housing issues affecting pregnancy, child care, and family health
Antenatal examination includes but is not limited to:	• Abdominal palpation to identify fetal lie and presentation • Measurement of fundal height and estimation of expected progression of pregnancy • Identification of all signs/ evidence of pregnancy • Documentation of findings from a physical examination and follow up according to procedures in manual
Information provided includes:	• Normal and abnormal vaginal discharge • Care of the perineum • PMTCT of HIV • Resumption of sexual relations • Obtaining baby clothes and nappies • Sources of advice and support
2. Potentially serious complications of pregnancy requiring referral may include:	• Vaginal bleeding (painful and painless)—threatened miscarriage, incomplete miscarriage, placenta previa, placental abruption • Abdominal pain in early pregnancy—ectopic pregnancy • Premature labor and premature rupture of membranes • Proteinuria/ hypertension—pregnancy-induced hypertension • Signs and symptoms of gestational diabetes • Other urinary abnormalities—urinary tract infections (UTIs), glucosuria • Reduced fetal movements and/or signs of poor fetal growth • Signs and symptoms such as: • Shortness of breath • A rise in BP • Rapid weight gain • Poor weight gain • Edema • Abnormal fundal heights for dates • Absence of fetal heartbeat • Anemia • Abnormal fetal lie (transverse, oblique)

Evidence Guide

Critical aspects of competence	Evidence should demonstrate the individual's ability to: • Undertake antenatal care • Provide information, guidance, and support to clients and their families on antenatal health issues • Provide physical examination of pregnant woman, identify and refer potential risky pregnancies

table continues next page

Variables	Range
Underpinning knowledge and attitudes	Essential knowledge must include: • Understanding organization policies and procedures relating to client confidentiality • Anatomy/ physiology, pharmacology, and abnormalities related to pregnancy • Knowledge of antenatal health and prevention of infection • Nutritional needs of pregnant women • Health conditions, obstetric problems, and associated issues related to pregnancy • Strategies to: • Improve antenatal health in the community • Address clients presenting with antenatal problems • Medical and obstetrics problems requiring referral • Relevant treatments, medicines, and associated care services available • Risks and contraindications associated with relevant treatments and medication • Realistic expectation of client condition during monitoring of progress
Underpinning skills	Essential skills must include the ability to: • Provide antenatal examination, identify pregnancy-related health problems and abnormalities, and inform the client • Conduct home visit and refer pregnant women with health problems • Conduct physical examination
Resource requirements	The following resources must be provided: • Workplace or fully equipped assessment location, including consumable materials • Approved assessment tools • Certified assessor/assessor's panel
Methods of assessment	Competence may be assessed through: • Practical assessment by direct observation of tasks through simulation/ role-play • Written exam/ test on underpinning knowledge • Questions or interview on underpinning knowledge • Project-related conditions (real or simulated) • Portfolio assessment (for example, log book from training providers or employers) Assessment methods must confirm the ability to access and correctly interpret and apply the essential underpinning knowledge.
Context for assessment	Competence may be assessed in the workplace or in a simulated workplace setting. This competence standard could be assessed on its own or in combination with other competencies relevant to the job function.

Source: Ethiopia Federal Ministry of Education, 2013.

TVET Program Structure for Health Extension Service Level III

table continues next page

Unit of Competence	Module Code & Title	Collecting, Maintaining, and Utilizing Community Health Data	Learning Outcomes	Duration (In Hours)		
				Theory	Practice	Total
HLT HES3 01 0213	Collect, Maintain, and Utilize Community Health Data	HLT HES3 M01 0213	• Plan and prepare the necessary materials for data collection • Collect data that need to be entered into the health database system • Collect vital events and surveillance data • Prepare and submit reports • Contribute to working with community to identify health needs	20	28	48
HLT HES3 02 0213	Perform Community Mobilization and Provide Health Education	HLT HES3 M02 0213	• Participate in the determination of community health information needs • Participate in the preparation of health information for use by the health worker assigned • Provide health promotion and education services • Train model families • Perform advocacy of identified health issues • Promote community mobilization on the identified health issues	38	84	122
HLT HES3 03 0213	Promote and Implement Hygiene and Environmental Health Services	HLT HES3 M03 0213	• Promote and provide environmental and personal hygiene education • Establish and demonstrate community-appropriate sanitation technologies • Provide environmental health service	40	80	120
HLT HES3 04 0213	Prevent and Control Common Communicable Diseases	HES3 M04 0213	• Educate the community on early detection and prevention of communicable diseases • Perform disease surveillance • Follow up cases	60	80	140
HLT HES3 05 0213	Prevent and Control Common Noncommunicable Diseases	HLT HES3 M05 0213	• Educate the community on healthy lifestyle and early detection of disease • Screen and refer clients requiring further investigation and management • Follow up cases and promote community-based rehabilitation	30	10	40

Unit of Competence	Module Code & Title		Learning Outcomes	Duration (In Hours)		
				Theory	Practice	Total
HLT HES3 06 0213	HLT HES3 M06 0213	Promoting Community Nutrition	• Collect appropriate information for preparing nutrition education • Provide basic nutrition information/ education to the clients • Monitor client response to the information/ education	30	50	80
HLT HES3 07 0213	HLT HES3 M07 0213	Promoting and Providing Antenatal Care	• Monitor client response to the information/ education • Conduct home visit and refer pregnant women with health problems	40	40	80
HLT HES3 08 0213	HLT HES3 M08 0213	Promoting Institutional Delivery and Providing Delivery Service	• Support women during childbirth • Provide normal delivery • Provide immediate neonatal care	40	140	180
HLT HES3 09 0213	HLT HES3 M09 0213	Promoting and Providing Postnatal Care	• Provide services for lactating mothers on infant care, nutrition, and exclusive breastfeeding • Organize and follow up maternal health programs	16	24	40
HLT HES3 10 0213	HLT HES3 M10 0213	Promoting Child Survival, Growth, and Development and Applying Integrated Community Case Management (ICCM)	• Promote child survival, growth, and development activities • Assess and manage common childhood illness • Refer children requiring further care	46	56	102
HLT HES3 11 0213	HLT HES3 M11 0213	Promoting and Implementing Immunization	• Plan immunization programs • Conduct immunization programs	40	80	120
HLT HES3 12 0213	HLT HES3 M12 0213	Promoting and Providing Family Planning Service	• Educate the community on family planning options • Educate adolescents on family planning and STI	40	70	110
HLT HES3 13 0213	HLT HES3 M13 0213	Promoting and Providing Adolescent and Youth Reproductive Health	• Plan adolescent and youth RH services • Promote adolescent and youth RH services • Provide RH service package • Register and document RH records	20	20	40

table continues next page

Unit of Competence	Module Code & Title		Learning Outcomes	Duration (In Hours)		
				Theory	Practice	Total
HLT HES3 14 0213	Provide First Aid	HLT HES3 M14 0213	Providing First Aid Service	• Assess and identify client's condition • Provide first aid service • Refer client requiring further care	20	70	90
HLT HES3 15 0213	Manage Community Health Service	HLT HES3 M15 0213	Managing Community Health Service	• Follow organizational guidelines, understand health policy and service delivery system • Work ethically • Provide team leadership and assign responsibilities • Establish quality standards, assess and record quality of service delivery • Manage work and resources at a health post • Lead workplace communication	20	20	20
HLT HES3 16 0213	Respond to Emergencies	HLT HES3 M18 0213	Responding to Emergencies	• Prepare for emergency situation • Evaluate the emergency • Act in an emergency • Apply essential first aid techniques	10	0	10
				Total in school	510	852	1,362
				Community attachment (internship)			320
				Grand total			**1,682**

Source: FMOH 2013b.

Note: The time duration (hours) indicated for the module should include all activities in and out of the training institution.

Example of Training Module for Health Extension Service Level III (Antenatal Care)

LEARNING MODULE 7	*Logo of TVET Provider*

TVET PROGRAM TITLE: **Health Extension Services Level III**
MODULE TITLE: **Promoting and Providing Antenatal Care**
MODULE CODE: **HLT HES3 M07 0213**
NOMINAL DURATION: **80 Hours**
MODULE DESCRIPTION: This module aims to provide the trainees with the knowledge, skills, and attitudes required to provide antenatal examination, and advise and conduct early referral of cases with abnormalities and/or complications during pregnancy and delivery.
LEARNING OUTCOMES: At the end of the module the learner will be able to: **LO1**. Provide antenatal examination and information for pregnant women **LO2**. Conduct home visit and refer pregnant women with risk factors
MODULE CONTENTS: **LO1**. Provide antenatal examination and information for pregnant women **1.1** Definition of terms **1.2** Introduction to anatomy and physiology of the female reproductive system **1.2.1.1** External female genitalia **1.2.1.2** Internal female reproductive organs **1.2.1.3** Anatomy of the female pelvis **1.2.1.4** The fetal skull 1.2.1.4.1. Fontanels and sutures of the fetal skull 1.2.1.4.2. Regions and landmarks in the fetal skull **1.3** Hormonal and physiological changes during pregnancy 1.3.1. Female reproductive hormones 1.3.2. Physiological changes during pregnancy **1.4** Fertilization and zygote implantation **1.5** Diagnosing pregnancy **1.5.1** Possible symptoms of pregnancy **1.5.2** Probable signs of pregnancy **1.5.3** Positive signs and symptoms of pregnancy **1.6** Focused antenatal care **1.6.1** Concepts and principles of focused antenatal care (FANC) **1.6.2** The antenatal care card **1.7** Promoting antenatal care **1.7.1** Health promotion, advocacy, and community mobilization **1.7.1.1** Nutrition during pregnancy

table continues next page

LEARNING MODULE 7	*Logo of TVET Provider*

1.7.1.2 Hygiene during pregnancy
1.7.1.3 Living a healthy lifestyle
1.7.1.4 Benefits of early and exclusive breastfeeding
1.7.1.5 Advocacy and community mobilization
1.7.1.5.1. Opinion leaders as advocates of antenatal care
1.7.1.5.2. Men as advocates of antenatal care
1.8 General assessment of the pregnant woman
1.8.1 Checking for signs and symptoms of malnutrition/ undernutrition
1.8.2 Checking her vital signs
1.9 Identifying possible risk factors in pregnancy
1.9.1 Pre-eclamsia and eclamsia
1.9.2 Multiparty
1.9.3 Multiple pregnancies
1.9.4 Anemia, diabetes, etc.
1.10 Estimating gestational age from fundal height measurement
1.10.1 Measuring the fundal height
1.11 Assessing the fetus
1.11.1 Finding the baby's position in the uterus
1.11.2 Inspecting and palpating the mother's abdomen
1.11.3 Listening/auscultation for the fetal heartbeat
1.12 Minor disorders of pregnancy and its management
1.13 Common medical disorders in pregnancy
LO2. Conduct home visit and refer pregnant woman with risk factors
2.1 Identifying risk factors
2.2 Refer mothers with risk factors
2.3 Home care visit

LEARNING METHODS:
- Lecture and discussion
- Role-play
- Group discussions
- Case discussions and seminars
- Demonstration (real or simulation)

ASSESSMENT METHODS:
Competence may be accessed through:
- Practical assessment
- Written exam/test
- Oral questioning
- Project work (real or simulation)

ASSESSMENT CRITERIA:
LO1. Provide antenatal examination and information for pregnant women
- General, social, and obstetric health history are taken and documented to deliver health care.
- Symptoms of pregnancy are identified. Antenatal care plan is prepared in consultation with the pregnant woman, based on the standard protocols and client requirements.
- Information on healthy living and maternal health risk factors are discussed.
- Antenatal examination is performed in line with the standard protocols and client requirements.
- Information on birthing options, signs of labor, and stages of labor, pain management techniques, and family attendance at delivery are provided for client.
- Sign and symptoms of minor disorders of pregnancy and potential serious complications are identified to provide advice and refer to the next level.
- Information is provided on PMTCT of HIV.
- Women are supported to obtain the necessary medicines and provided with appropriate information on use.

table continues next page

LEARNING MODULE 7	Logo of TVET Provider

LO2. Conduct home visit and refer pregnant women with risk factors

- Registers of women undergoing antenatal care are maintained according to the organizational policies and procedures.
- Schedules of participation in antenatal care and use are kept to organize the continuing care for women.
- Reminders and other assistance are organized and/or provided to women to attend antenatal care according to their needs.
- Referral and communication networks with medical staff, midwives, allied health staff, birthing facilities, and female community elders are maintained.
- Records on attendance for antenatal care and birthing outcomes are kept and used to follow antenatal care.

Source: FMOH 2013c.

Selected Results on HEWs Competency, Based on HEP Midterm Evaluation

Areas where HEWs have relatively better knowledge:

- Antenatal care: Knowledge in use of antenatal care was relatively high—preparation for birth and disease prevention (68 percent), promotion of safe delivery (59.8 percent), detection of existing diseases and management of complications (52.2 percent), ensuring women have an individualized birth plan (51.1 percent), and breastfeeding promotion (17.4 percent).
- Family planning: Majority of HEWs would provide information about all methods (76.0 percent), benefits (63.3 percent), risks (57.0 percent), and effectiveness (57.0 percent) of family planning methods.
- Childhood illnesses (identifying ARI, diarrhea management, uncomplicated malaria): Nearly two-thirds of HEWs mentioned cough, fever, and fast/ difficulty breathing as signs of ARI. Majority of HEWs stated that they would give more fluids (80 percent) and continue to feed the child (64 percent) when he or she has diarrhea. The signs and symptoms of malaria mentioned were high temperature (82 percent), headache (80 percent), chills/ shivering (78 percent), poor appetite (63 percent), vomiting (52 percent), and joint pain (48 percent).

Areas where HEWs have relatively poor knowledge:

- Labor establishment: The first step for HEWs in assisting delivery is establishing a woman is in labor. The important signs they are expected to look for include regular uterine contraction associated with cervical dilatation and pain. The responses were 53 percent for regular uterine contraction, 53 percent for cervical dilatation, and 40 percent for pain.
- Labor monitoring: The responses of HEWs for optimal labor monitoring were 49.0 percent for measurement of fetal heart rate, 53.0 percent for assessment of cervical dilatation, 33.0 percent for descent of head, 3.5 percent for uterine contraction, 14.0 percent for degree of molding, and 46.0 percent for maternal blood pressure.

- Assessing a mother with vaginal bleeding: HEWs were given a case study of a pregnant woman who presented with vaginal bleeding at 34 weeks of gestation. They were asked to list the signs to look for and the actions they would take. Percentage of HEWs stating that they would look for the most important danger signs are 34 percent for signs of anemia, 26 percent for signs of shock, 23 percent for amount of external bleeding, and 15 percent for abdominal tenderness.

- Newborn care: HEWs were asked to list the immediate care they give to newborns while attending to a delivery. The responses of HEWs in order of frequency were to initiate breastfeeding within one hour (54.0 percent), to wipe the face after birth of the head (52.9 percent), to ensure baby is breathing (51.8 percent), to provide cord care with sterile cut 4 to 6 centimeters from umbilicus (50.4 percent), to provide thermal protection (47.2 percent), to weigh the baby (37.4 percent), to assess/ examine newborn within one hour (12.3 percent), and to administer eye prophylaxis (11.2 percent).

- Integrated management of childhood illness (IMCI): Only less than a quarter of HEWs stated they would integrate vaccination services, nutritional counseling, and growth monitoring.

References

CNHDE (Center for National Health Development in Ethiopia). 2012. "Evaluation of Health Extension Program, Rural Ethiopia 2010." Addis Ababa.

CSA (Central Statistical Agency). 2011. "Ethiopia Demographic and Health Survey 2000." Addis Ababa.

———. 2012a. "2011 National Statistics (Abstract)." Addis Ababa.

———. 2012b. "Ethiopia Welfare Monitoring Survey 2011." Addis Ababa.

———. 2006. "Ethiopia Demographic and Health Survey 2005." CSA and ICF International, Addis Ababa and Calverton, MD.

———. 2012. "Ethiopia Demographic and Health Survey 2011." CSA and ICF International, Addis Ababa, and Calverton, MD.

Federal Ministry of Education. 2013. "Health Extension Service—Occupational Standard for Level III." Addis Ababa.

Feysa, Berhanu, Christopher Herbst, Wuleta Lemma, and Agnes Soucat. 2012. *The Health Workforce in Ethiopia: Addressing the Remaining Challenges*. Washington, DC: World Bank.

FMOH (Federal Ministry of Health). 2004. "Annual Performance Report EFY1997." Addis Ababa

———. 2005. "Annual Performance Report EFY1998."

———. 2006. "Annual Performance Report EFY1999."

———. 2007a. "Annual Performance Report EFY2000."

———. 2007b "Health Extension Program in Ethiopia —Profile." Addis Ababa.

———. 2008a. "Annual Performance Report EFY2001."

———. 2008b. "Health Insurance Strategy." Addis Ababa.

———. 2009. "Annual Performance Report EFY2002."

———. 2010a. "Annual Performance Report EFY2003."

———. 2010b. "Ethiopia's Fourth National Health Accounts, 2007/2008." Addis Ababa

———. 2010c. "Health Sector Development Program IV (HSDP-IV) 2010/11–2014/15." Addis Ababa.

———. 2012a. "Annual Performance Report EFY2004."

———. 2012b. "Health Extension Program Implementation Guideline" (Revised). Addis Ababa.

———. 2012c. "Presentations on Progress in CBHI Pilots." Addis Ababa

————. 2013a. "Annual Performance Report EFY2005."

————. 2013b. "Annual Performance Report EFY2005." Special Bulletin.

————. 2013c. "Ethiopia TVET system Model Curriculum—Health Extension Service Level III." Adama.

————. 2014. "Ethiopia's Fifth National Health Accounts, 2010/2011." Addis Ababa

FMOH, UNICEF, UNFPA, WHO, and AMDD. 2010. "Ethiopia National Baseline Assessment for Emergency Obstetric and Newborn Care 2008." Addis Ababa.

Government of Ethiopia, Proclamation No. 690/2010. Social Health Insurance Proclamation, p. 5494.

MOFED (Ministry of Finance and Economic Development). 2010. "Growth and Transformation Plan (2010/11–2014/15) Volume I Main Text." Addis Ababa.

Nejmudin, Bilal, Christopher Herbst, Feng Zhao, Agnes Soucat, and Christophe Lemiere. 2011. "Health Extension Workers in Ethiopia: Improved Access and Coverage for the Rural Poor." In *Yes Africa Can: Success Stories from a Dynamic Continent*, edited by Punam Chuhan-Pole and Manka Angwafo. Washington, DC: World Bank.

Purvis, George, Abebe Alebachew, and Wondwossen Feleke. 2011. "Ethiopia Health Sector Financing Project Mid-Term Evaluation Summary Report." U.S. Agency for International Development (USAID), Addis Ababa.

Rutstein, S. 1999. "Wealth versus Expenditure: Comparison between the DHS Wealth Index and Household Expenditures in Four Departments of Guatemala." (Unpublished, ORC Macro, Calverton, MD).

Solar, O., and A. Irwin. 2010. "A Conceptual Framework for Action on the Social Determinants of Health." Social Determinants of Health Discussion Paper 2 (Policy and Practice). World Health Organization, Geneva.

United Nations Inter-agency Group for Child Mortality Estimation (UN-IGME). 2013. "Levels and Trends in Child Mortality." UN-IGME.

World Bank. 2012a. *Ethiopia Economic Update —Overcoming Inflation, Raising Competitiveness.* Addis Ababa: World Bank.

World Bank. 2012b. "Ethiopia Health Millineum Development Goals Program-for-Results Project Appraisal Document." World Bank.

————. 2013. "Ethiopia Promotion of Basic Services Phase III Project Appraisal Document." World Bank.

ECO-AUDIT

Environmental Benefits Statement

The World Bank Group is committed to reducing its environmental footprint. In support of this commitment, the Publishing and Knowledge Division leverages electronic publishing options and print-on-demand technology, which is located in regional hubs worldwide. Together, these initiatives enable print runs to be lowered and shipping distances decreased, resulting in reduced paper consumption, chemical use, greenhouse gas emissions, and waste.

The Publishing and Knowledge Division follows the recommended standards for paper use set by the Green Press Initiative. The majority of our books are printed on Forest Stewardship Council (FSC)–certified paper, with nearly all containing 50–100 percent recycled content. The recycled fiber in our book paper is either unbleached or bleached using totally chlorine free (TCF), processed chlorine free (PCF), or enhanced elemental chlorine free (EECF) processes.

More information about the Bank's environmental philosophy can be found at http://crinfo.worldbank.org/wbcrinfo/node/4.